EMDR Up Close:

Subtleties of Trauma Processing

EMDR Up Close:

Subtleties of Trauma Processing

Philip Manfield, Ph.D.

www.philipmanfield.com

This book was originally set in 12 point Times New Roman and printed and bound by CreateSpace, a DBA of On-Demand Publishing, LLC, an Amazon.com company.

Copyright © 2013 by Philip Manfield

10 9 8 7 6 5 4 3 2 1

All rights reserved. Printed in the United States of America. No part of this book may be used or reproduced in any manner whatsoever without written permission from Philip Manfield except in the case of brief quotations in reviews for inclusion in a magazine, newspaper, or broadcast.

Library of Congress Cataloging-in-Publication Data

Manfield, Philip
    EMDR Up Close: Subtleties of Trauma Processing/ by Philip Manfield.
 p. cm.
Third Edition
 Includes bibliographical references.
 ISBN 1492399620

1. Psychotherapy. 2. Attachment Disorder--Treatment. 3. EMDR 4. Eye Movement Desensitization and Reprocessing
5. Trauma--Treatment 6. Trauma—Therapy 7. Personality disorders--Treatment. 8. attachment disorder--Treatment. 9. Narcissism--Treatment. 10. Schizoid
 personality—Treatment 11. Memory Reconsolidation.
I. Title.

EAN-13 9781492399620

 for Library of Congress

Cover photo by www.istockphoto.com– All rights reserved.

Originally manufactured in the United States of America. Philip Manfield offers other books and DVD's For information, visit www.philipmanfield.com

To My Mother,
Roslyn Manfield

Contents

Acknowledgements
Introduction

Section I: Straightforward EMDR
Chapter 1: New Twists: Ideas and Terms that May Be
    Unfamiliar   1
Chapter 2: The Right Target Goes a Long Way   31
Chapter 3: Simple Processing With A Good Target   49

Section II: Complexity in Targeting and Processing
Chapter 4: Using Resourcing to Help Get to the Target   63
Chapter 5: Floatback to Four Years Old   101
Chapter 6: Inadequate Preparation   127
Chapter 7: Getting the Right Floatback   155
Chapter 8: Getting the Target Right   173
References   181
About the Author   187

Acknowledgements

I am deeply indebted to those who have encouraged me to undertake this project. In particular, my friend and colleague Dr. Lewis Engel has provided invaluable encouragement, observations and insights throughout this process. He has both watched videos with me and provided sage advice, and also read each chapter as it was completed, suggesting technical, professional and editorial revisions. Special thanks to Dr. Carol Odsess, who has viewed scores of my demo videos with me. She has offered invaluable suggestions about clinical principals and techniques the videos illustrate and has also helped me decide which videos would be most valuable for inclusion in this book. For editorial help, my thanks too go to Alison Lingo. And very special thanks to Marianne Ault-Riche, MFT and Linda Dackman, both of whom could not bear the thought of this book circulating with numerous typos and took it upon themselves to identify the bulk of them.

Thanks also to my brother, David Manfield, a clinical psychologist in Portland, Oregon; my friend and colleague Isabelle Avril Pronovost in Quebec City, Canada; and to Claudia Locsin, LMFT and Duncan Bennett, Ph.D for taking the time to read and comment on the writing of this volume as it evolved. Special thanks to Miriam Garcia, Naomi Reines and Renee Hikiji at the Continuing

Educaton Division of John F. Kennedy University for supporting me in my EMDR training program there and for contributing to the phenomenal success of that program. I am particularly grateful to them for creating the JFKU on-line EMDR video library (www.emdrvideos.com).

Finally, none of these projects would have taken place without the powerful creativity and clinical acumen that went into the development of this incredible treatment method. There are so many days that I watch a client walk out of my office after a particularly dramatic life-changing session, and I feel priviledged to have participated in such a deep healing. Often, at those times, I take a deep breath and say to myself, "Thank you, Francine Shapiro."

Introduction

I have been conducting EMDR Basic Trainings through John F. Kennedy University Division of Continuing Education and other institutions for more than a decade now. I have facilitated at EMDR trainings for a decade before that. The position of EMDR in the psychotherapy world and the way it is practiced has undergone a transformation during that period of time. In the beginning, participants in EMDR trainings expressed concern that they might be viewed as unprofessional or "fringy" for conducting EMDR. At most trainings there was even someone who was concerned about being accused of malpractice. Now, when I go around the room at the beginning of trainings and ask people to indicate their particular reason for enrolling, there are usually quite a few who say that they have seen the impressive results colleagues are producing with EMDR, and have come to believe it might be unethical not to offer EMDR.

EMDR started as a technique for processing trauma within a variety of other broader treatment approaches. The primary use was to process single incident traumas, and the bulk of initial research was intended to evaluate this use. Now, its application has broadened considerably and it has matured into a sophisticated approach to treatment of a wide range of conditions. Research, however, has still been primarily focused on single incident traumas. While we rely on

Shapiro's seminal text (Shapiro 1995, 2001) to define the way EMDR is conducted, the scope of that text is limited by the range of issues it addresses as well as it's being more than a decade old and therefore lacking commentary about more recent developments.

On-line Library of Clinical Videos

The EMDR trainings I teach have also changed over the years. In 1999, I participated in providing a five day EMDR Part I training in Turkey three months after a major earthquake there. The training began with a video of a full session of EMDR conducted a week prior to the training with a Turkish woman who had been traumatized by the earthquake. Seeing that video transformed the attitudes about EMDR of the 150 training attendees from *skeptical* to *convinced*. Because of that experience, I began to show a video at the beginning of each EMDR Basic Training I conducted illustrating a complete EMDR treatment taking place in a single session. Soon after that, I added a video session at the beginning of Part II trainings as well. I also included at least one live demonstration session in each part of the training. Student feedback consistently indicated that the experiences of viewing these sessions were extremely helpful in enabling them to integrate what they were learning into a cohesive model of EMDR.

In recent years I have responded to this feedback by offering the option to students of watching videos during lunch one or both days of the weekend. Again, the positive feedback was consistent. Students also wanted to know how they could watch other clinical videos of EMDR. A thread of similar sentiment recently appeared on the EMDRIA-Approved Consultants' Listserv in which consultants indicated how useful clinical videos would be for learning EMDR and how little was available. The Continuing Education division of John F. Kennedy University (JFKU) responded by offering to construct a website for practicing psychotherapists devoted to EMDR clinical videos. Initially consisting of more than twenty five videos of my EMDR work, it is hoped that additional videos will be added over time to make this an increasingly rich resource for practicing EMDR clinicians and newly trained EMDR practitioners as well. The videos from which the transcripts in this book were made are almost all among those included in the collection being offered by JFKU. Note that numbers at the beginning of chapters (i.e. "Video #16") represent the notation for the corresponding video number in the on-line JFKU video library. For clinicians who would like to view a few videos without registering for the entire collection, I have created a free website, *www.emdrvideo.com*. Made from demonstrations at my trainings, full permission to use them in this way has been obtained.

Most of what is discussed in *EMDR Up Close* is not new, although some content may have been only recently added to some EMDR trainings. Nevertheless, the transcripts in this book follow fairly closely the EMDR protocol as originally defined by Shapiro (1995, 2001). When a deviation from that protocol occurrs, I have tried to note it and explain the reason for it.

What is perhaps different about the way I conduct EMDR is the standard I apply to the Assessment Phase (Phase III) and to the Desensitization and Reprocessing Phase (Phase IV). For complex targets, I frequently spend half a session getting the cognitions and the entire Assessment phase right. (The discussion of Memory Reconsolidation in Chapter One of this volume helps to clarify the importance of doing this.) When the Desensitization and Reprocessing Phase finally begins, however, it tends to be clean and focused, and adaptive resolution occurs relatively rapidly. If Desensitization and Reprocessing is not progressing as expected, I believe there is always a reason. One can usually figure out what it is and how to correct it.

Two Categories of Sessions

The focus of the EMDR sessions included in this volume fall primarily into one of two categories, relatively complex issues with origins in early childhood or *low-hanging fruit*. The concept of low-hanging fruit is discussed extensively in Chapter One and elsewhere in this volume. Simply put, targets that constitute low-hanging fruit are those that are straightforward and can be expected to be resolved in a single session. Examples might be single incident traumas and blocked grieving. The low-hanging fruit demonstrations occur in Part I after the class has had an extensive discussion of this subject, and students have been encouraged to offer examples of such targets belonging to themselves or their clients. We discuss and evaluate each proposed example of low-hanging fruit. Then I ask if someone is willing to volunteer to process their target in a demonstration. It should be no surprise that these demonstrations tend to be relatively brief and uncomplicated. They serve as a reminder of how EMDR works when it goes smoothly.

The other category of video sessions is instructive in illustrating ways to overcome various complications to EMDR processing. These demonstrations occur after a discussion of techniques for finding feeder memories and touchstone events. A short group exercise in which I ask class members to locate a mildly disturbing recent memory and then "float back" to a related early memory follows. The clients appearing in these videos are chosen from the handful of participants in a training who were unable to successfully float back to an early memory. Those who have difficulty with the floatback exercise tend to be those who have a more extensive trauma history or who have a relatively challenging presenting issue. These sessions illustrate relatively sophisticated techniques for identifying touchstone memories that can be processed effectively with EMDR.

Idiosyncratic Aspects of the Sessions in This Volume

The actual process taking place in the sessions in this volume is typical of many sessions I might conduct in my practice. In these sessions, however, there are probably more demand characteristics arising from this situation in front of a class than in a standard therapy session, so clients tend to be more motivated to come to a successful resolution and possibly to exaggerate the benefits of the session. Readers will need to judge that for themselves. Because of this risk, I do, when practical, double check my work by quizzing clients during the session about the nature of the apparent resolution and about whether specific triggers that were mentioned in the session remain active.

Unlike some of the clients in my private practice, most of these clients are functioning fairly well in their lives, well enough at least to become licensed clinicians. Consequently, most do not require resourcing before trauma processing, so the particular EMDR skills illustrated by these sessions include primarily those used in the "Assessment" and "Desensitization and Reprocessing" Phases (Phases III and IV), with little attention to the "Preparation" Phase (Phase II) where resourcing would normally take place. Resourcing transcripts and explanations are confined to my earlier book, *Dyadic Resourcing: Creating a Foundation for Processing Trauma*, as is a discussion of history taking and case conceptualization (Phase I). In other words, the earlier book is focused on Phases I and II, and this volume is focused on III and IV.

Sessions transcribed for this book were usually conducted under more restrictive time pressures than that of a normal clinical EMDR session. As a result, I do not take proper histories with these clients, nor do extensive preparation. I also tend to be more active in offering suggestions to them and in intervening sooner with cognitive interweaves. In reviewing videos of these sessions, I also noted that I was making occasional mirroring or clarifying comments between sets that I would not normally do, probably a compensation for not having had time to establish rapport. I also noticed myself moving sessions along by frequently completing clients' sentences, something that I do not normally do.

I am interested in how highly experienced EMDR practitioners conduct EMDR, how closely they adhere to the protocol, and when and how they diverge from it. I believe that most of the ways in which I diverge are typical of other clinicians. One area of divergence is that I offer clients suggestions in formulating a target, suggestions about what sort of touchstone memory might be involved, and suggestions for negative and positive cognitions. Although not a break from the protocol, these active suggestions are not encouraged by Shapiro (1995, 2001); she emphasizes letting clients come up with their own cognitions.

When I was first trained in EMDR, I tried to restrain my suggestions to clients. I remember sometimes spending whole sessions trying to help a client arrive at a suitable Negative Cognition and opposite Positive Cognition without introducing my own suggestions. In many cases, the session felt wasted because little progress was made. Coming up with the right cognitions was difficult at first even for me, having had very little training in cognitive therapy at the time, but it was sometimes nearly impossible for clients who had not even had training in psychology.

The pitfall to the therapist's playing a more active role in making these suggestions is that the therapist may be wrong and the client might accept a suggestion that does not really fit. I have seen this occur in videos of session conducted by very experienced EMDR therapists, and I have also seen it a few times in the videos included in this collection. However, I have not found instances in this volume where it appeared to lead the session astray or harm the client. One piece of advice that I offer trainees and adhere to myself to prevent this is to provide clients with a menu of possibilities as opposed to a single suggestion.

The way I practice EMDR that is probably different from the way many others do is that I work very hard to find the right target and then to identify all of its important facets. I imagine that some EMDR practitioners with a more *laissez faire* attitude might find my approach to be *needlessly* bogged down in structure and precision. They might even perceive me as badgering the client. My style of conducting EMDR fits with how I think, and it may not be right for everyone. If the reader finds this style to be somewhat foreign I hope he or she will observe how it plays out in multiple sessions before rejecting it outright and consider the possible benefit of incorporating some aspects of it into his or her own style. Over the years, I've provided consultation to many hundreds of EMDR clinicians, and most find that this tighter approach to targeting and processing that I am suggesting makes processing of difficult targets and working with difficult clients more orderly and effective.

In the Assessment Phase (Phase III) the critical skills are finding the appropriate "Touchstone Event" and determining the cognitive distortion (negative cognition) introduced by that event. In most of the sessions that have been included in this volume, approximately half of the session is devoted to obtaining what I term a "crisp" target. Once Desensitization and Reprocessing begins, processing is normally very rapid, so that most of these sessions require little more than a half hour, with approximately fifteen minutes devoted to resolving the disturbance once Phase IV begins. Characteristic of the way the processing phase is conducted is a heightened discrimination between associations that represent processing and associations that do not. Clients can become stuck and begin looping due to cognitive blocks, but I also emphasize in this volume the roles of defense, digression, and general divergence from the target in interfering with processing.

Limitations of a Demonstration Session

I have at times questioned the appropriateness of conducting a demonstration that differs in important ways from what I am teaching the class. I teach the benefits of taking a thorough trauma-informed history, evaluating the client's readiness for EMDR trauma processing, and providing preparation and resourcing. In the demonstrations, on the other hand, I sit down in front of a class cold with a "client" whom I usually do not know, and we begin to talk about a target or symptom with the intention of finding a touchstone memory responsible for that symptom, and then possibly processing it with EMDR. The feedback I am given by consultees and trainees, however, is that seeing these demonstrations gives them a more solid model for how to conduct an EMDR session, and gives them confidence that EMDR works. In many cases, trainees express surprise at seeing an aspect of the protocol conducted in a particular way, even though what they are seeing is exactly what they have just been taught. Hearing and seeing are very different ways of learning.

Please Note: For completeness, I have included many remarks in the introduction of this book that duplicate comments from the introduction of, *Dyadic Resourcing*. If that information is still fresh for you, I apologize for the redundancy, and suggest you skip ahead to Chapter One

Practice Does Not Always Make Perfect

As I began writing the first book in this series, *Dyadic Resourcing: Creating a Foundation for Processing Trauma* (Manfield, 2010), a friend and colleague mentioned an adage to me: "Practice does not make perfect; perfect practice makes perfect." Just as clinical consultation makes more perfect practice possible, I hope that both this book and that one will help readers make their EMDR practice more precise and more effective. In addition, it may also open up possibilities for using EMDR effectively with a wider variety of cases.

Nearly from the beginning, the development of EMDR has been guided by the principle of using as a model the sessions in which EMDR works well, and then, when processing does not seem to be progressing well, asking what is different about this process from those processes that worked. The cognitive interweave was developed as a way to jumpstart processing when it had stalled. Dr. Francine Shapiro, the innovator of EMDR, noticed (1995, 2001) that during successful EMDR processing, distortions relating to responsibility, safety and choice seemed to be addressed in that order. She reasoned that if one of these distortions was not resolving, it would be necessary to facilitate the resolution of that distortion and then the others would resolve in turn.

Introduction   xiii

EMDR Up Close presents sample sessions of clinical processes that work, transcripts of complete successful treatment sessions. It addresses clinical issues in these sessions on the most basic level: the way the therapist interprets the client's comments, the effects of the particular words the therapist uses, analysis of what precisely is preventing the client from moving forward, and discussions of the solutions available to the therapist in each situation. On the one hand, the volume will be useful for therapists who have mastered the basics of EMDR and now know enough to recognize some of the areas in which they need more information or training. On the other hand, it will be useful for EMDR clinicians practicing what they have learned imperfectly, and EMDR-trained clinicians whose training from many years back did not include many of the advancements developed only after they were trained. Finally, for newly trained EMDR therapists and seasoned clinicians as well, it will provide many models of EMDR sessions that work.

There is no substitution for experience and good clinical consultation. This book and *Dyadic Resourcing*, however, should help. In them, I discuss many of the issues that arise repeatedly in my clinical case consultation groups. Therapists use both their successes and failures in actual clinical practice to improve their craft; I hope that viewing or reading clinical sessions in this book will provide much of the same benefit as clinical experience, but have the added advantage that these sessions were selected for inclusion because they are particularly instructive. Unlike live demonstrations, these sessions are not happening in real time, so it is possible to stop frequently and discuss the details of what is taking place in the transcriptions, as well as to discuss the clinical issues involved.

Picking Up Where the Training Leaves Off

This book is not intended as an EMDR manual. It does not replace Shapiro's *Eye Movement Desensitization and Reprocessing: Basic Principles and Protocols* (1995, 2001). This book and its sequel complement that text by addressing in depth a variety of additional practical clinical situations that arise when therapists practice EMDR.

Clinicians newly trained in EMDR often struggle to begin using EMDR and integrating it into their practices. They usually do not have many clients coming for treatment because of suffering from single incident traumas. Clinicians want to first learn to use EMDR with relatively easy clients, but they may not have easy clients in their practices. Many are naturally hesitant because they feel like novices in EMDR, and they are accustomed to being experts. Their clients expect them to be experts. So, it is tempting to fall back on therapeutic approaches that they have used for years, and in which they have become expert. But, often these older practices are far from perfect in comparison to a clinical approach that can reliably produce superior results in less time.

So, how do clinicians make the transition from being trained to being expert, given the issues that prevent them from integrating EMDR into their practices? The recent inclusion of ten hours of required consultation as part of the basic EMDR training is a positive step in the direction of increased utilization of EMDR by providing clinical guidance beyond the classroom setting. This book is similarly intended to help clinicians, even those who have held off from actively using EMDR in their practices, to achieve greater expertise and confidence in conducting EMDR.

I suggest a triage approach when beginning to use EMDR. I suggest that the very minimum a clinician do is to take a thorough trauma-informed history. As does Shapiro (1995, 2001), I recommend beginning this process by asking for a list of the client's Top 10 most disturbing memories. I add to this a recommendation that clinicians ask for a list of the client's Top 10 best memories. I tell trainees that whether or not they actually conduct EMDR with a client, the treatment will be facilitated by obtaining this information. Any clinician, no matter how cautious about utilizing EMDR, can take this minimal initial step, especially if structured to prevent clients from becoming unduely activated. I tell clients, "I'm just looking for the headlines; I can get the stories later when we are ready to process them." After obtaining this history, which is the first Phase of the EMDR's 8-phases, a clinician has the option of returning to a more traditional psychotherapeutic approach or proceeding to Phase II of the EMDR procedure (Preparation). Taking a history will be beneficial whether or not EMDR is utilized in the treatment. (Note: history-taking and case conceptualization are the focus of Section I of my earlier book).

After obtaining a trauma-informed history from a variety of clients, clinicians are likely to notice that for some clients there are simple single-incident traumas that are likely to lend themselves to uncomplicated EMDR trauma processing and also positive memories that would be excellent focuses for resourcing. If possible, I recommend beginning with the low-hanging fruit. Shapiro's book (1995, 2001) contains many warnings about how improper use of EMDR can hurt clients; I find that many clinicians who read the book become anxious about using EMDR, lest, as neophytes, they might hurt their clients. For these clinicians, I suggest beginning with resourcing. Resourcing involves most of the clinical skills that are useful for EMDR trauma processing, but a timid clinician need not be concerned that unsuccessful resourcing might cause harm to a client. Resourcing takes place during Phase II of EMDR (Preparation), and a particular form of resourcing, Dyadic Resourcing, is the primary focus of Section II of my earlier book by that name.

Practical Clinical Examples

Along with its companion volume, *Dyadic Resourcing: Creating a Foundation for Processing Trauma* (Manfield, 2010), this book's clinical and conceptual detail illustrate concretely recommendations for using EMDR to address both simple and complex cases. I have written it at the urging of clinicians whom I have trained and others who have consulted with me. Much of the material stems directly from training and consultation sessions. Many experienced clinicians will already have been using some of the techniques described in this book. For them, I would hope the book confirms the efficacy of what they are already doing, while occasionally offering a new way of looking at an old concept or suggesting new applications for time-tested techniques. I hope that for some it explains in relatively precise terms what they have already been doing intuitively, or adds to the diversity of their available tools. Other readers will find that this book offers concrete clinical examples of some of the concepts that were taught in the training, and suggests practical ways to implement EMDR with a wide variety of clients.

My Backgound

When I began using EMDR in 1991, I had been an analytical therapist for many years and an eclectic, psychodynamic therapist for many years before that. My first book, *Split Self/ Split Object: Understanding and Treating Borderline, Narcissistic and Schizoid Disorders* (Manfield, 1992), was in press. I identified strongly with the role of the learner. I had written that book because the process of learning and integrating concepts of object relations, self-psychology, and James Masterson's approach to treating personality disorders had been complex and challenging for me. I thought if I presented this material in a concrete clinical context I could make it more accessible to other clinicians. The comments I received from readers have confirmed the need for this kind of teaching. Even today, more than two decades after the first publication of that book, I am stopped in elevators and hallways at conferences by clinicians who want me to know how useful that book has been for them.

It was in this spirit that I wrote my first two EMDR books, *EMDR Casebook* (Manfield, 2002) and *Dyadic Resourcing: Creating a Foundation for Processing Trauma* (Manfield, 2010), both focusing strongly on clinical phenomena. The latter relied on clinical transcripts and commentary, with a relatively small amount of didactic material added to give an overview. The response to the book among clinicians has been overwhelming both here, in North America, and on just about

Introduction   xvii

every other continent. It has confirmed for me that teaching through example can bring about the deepest learning. With this in mind, John F. Kennedy University has created a website (www.emdrclinicalvideos.com) devoted to providing video examples of EMDR trauma processing and resourcing. Currently the site contains in excess of 25 videos, including most of the videos from which the transcripts in this volume and my previous one were made. This video library is open to all licensed psychotherapists who will pay a small maintenance fee for unlimited access for three months. It can be accessed through www.emdrclinicalvideos.com. The title page of each clinical chapter of this book identifies the particular video in JFKU's site from which the transcript for that chapter was made.

Although my clinical background was diverse when I was first trained in EMDR, some of the essential concepts involved in practicing EMDR were new to me then. In particular, the cognitive portion of EMDR seemed cumbersome and I only became comfortable with it over time. On the other hand, my training in Object Relations, Reichian therapy (somatic), Gestalt, Transactional Analysis, Self Acceptance Training, Family Systems, Neuro-Linguistic Programming (NLP), Hypnosis, Eidetic psychotherapy, and Eastern religion, all seemed to fit in seemlessly with EMDR and enriched my ability to practice it.

Complexity of Giving Proper Credit

I expect that various techniques in this book will seem familiar to many readers. In some cases, it may be clear where these techniques originated, but many of the techniques are common to a variety of therapeutic approaches. Although I would like to give credit to the originators of the techniques that I employ, I may only be able to indicate from whom I learned them. Similarly, I have borrowed ideas from other EMDR therapists. Many of these ideas and techniques were developed simultaneously by more than one therapist; some people attribute those ideas to one clinician and others to another. Much of what I do, however, feels to me internally like it is mine; I have made it my own, although I know that it has very likely been borrowed from a variety of sources. What is hopefully new and unique in this book is the integration and presentation of the material. My intent is to make concepts and practical applications of those concepts accessible to as many clinicians as possible. Although, as I have stated before, this book is intended as a companion to its predecessor, it is designed to stand on its own.

Clinical Transcripts

If a transcript is not introduced as a reconstructed transcript, it can be assumed to be verbatim. In either case, the symbol "<><>" is used to indicate some form of alternating bilateral stimulation (BLS) — either eye movements, tones or vibrating pulsers (or tapping). Even if not explicitly printed in the transcripts, BLS is normally preceded in the session by the instruction, "Focus on that," and ends with, "Take a deep breath and blank it out. What's coming up now?"

As a matter of course, I usually offer to videotape my clients' sessions. The video is recorded on an SDHC memory card, which the client brings with him or her to the session, and takes home at the end of the session. I encourage clients to review the video recording of the previous session before coming to the next session. I have found the process of making these videos to be extraordinarily helpful to many of my clients. To some clients, these video recordings have been so helpful to treatment that I think the making of video recordings of sessions should be considered a standard of care. Those video recordings, however, belong to my clients, and I do not ask for permission to archive or show them. This is why the video material represented in this book comes from classroom demonstrations. The results that I see in my office, however, are comparable to those achieved during these demonstration sessions.

Introduction

The Commentary

It is recommended that for each transcript in this book, the reader first read through the entire session without reading the commentary, so that he or she can obtain an overall sense of the session. I think it will be helpful to obtain a sense of the emotional tone and shape of these sessions before reading the commentary and analyzing the processes involved. I have been told that many of the transcripts seem simple at first pass. When they are analyzed in the commentary, however, the subtle challenges and choice points that are involved become more apparent.

My commentary is, in most cases, merely my opinion without research validation. This book is about clinical skills. When clinical techniques are successful in achieving our desired therapeutic goal, we tend to use them. When they are not, we don't. The degree of efficacy in most cases is readily apparent, and I have included long-term follow-up from most of the clients to confirm the effectiveness of their sessions.

He / She, His / Her

For simplicity, I have referred to clients in the female gender in this book, unless the gender of the client is established by the transcript being discussed. To clearly distinguish the pronoun referents, I have referred to therapists in the male gender. I also occasionally refer to myself as "the therapist" or in the male third person.

xxxxxxxxxxxxxxxxxxxxxxxxxxxxxxxxxxxx

I learn best through example; I believe many other people do as well. While it's useful to hear a practitioner's explanation of why his or her work was effective, I think it's also commonly true of clinicians that at least part of their effectiveness arises out of things they do intuitively which they may not even be aware they are doing. I had the pleasure about fifteen years ago of accompanying my friend and colleague Jim Knipe to Turkey for a Humanitarian Assistance Program (HAP) project to train Turkish therapists in EMDR after the August 1999 Sea of Marmara earthquake there. Most memorable for me from that trip was the week Jim and I spent before the training began as we observed each other conducting EMDR with Turkish earthquake victims through translators. I learned a lot from watching Jim work, but was fascinated to hear that many of the aspects of Jim's work that I found most innovative and helpful he himself had not considered creative or unique. This may point out the value of clinicians observing the work of other clinicians whenever possible, either directly through video recordings or indirectly through transcripts, such as the ones in this volume. I believe that the potential of EMDR as an agent of change is indeed awesome, and I hope that the transcriptions and commentary in this book will help readers to deepen their ability to utilize this powerful tool.

Section I:

Straightforward EMDR

1

New Twists: Ideas and Terms that May Be Unfamiliar

Although most of what is in this volume is not new to EMDR, some of it is relatively new to EMDR trainings, and some of it is idiosyncratic to the EMDR trainings that I conduct. Rather than repeatedly interrupt the flow when these come up in the transcripts in this book, I will attempt to explain these ideas, techniques and concepts in this initial chapter and simply reference this chapter when they are referred to later in the book.

Memory Reconsolidation
MOUSE Without PTSD

The importance of Ringing The Bell

In the past decade, the science of neurology, as it relates to memory, has made a big leap forward, refuting a widely held misconception. For at least half a century, neuroscientists believed that memories linked to powerful emotion could not be extinguished. (McGaugh, J. L., & Roozendaal, B. ,2002; McGaugh, J. L. 1989) This belief was established through experiments with animal conditioning and human subjects. Traditional psychotherapeutic approaches of talking about the memory rationally and understanding that it is just a memory only masked or obscured the emotions linked to the memories. (Bouton, M.E. ,2004) These approaches sometimes gave the appearance of relief; but after treatment, the memory they dealt with was still active and the pain accompanying it could be reactivated by reminding the subject about the original memory. Scientists believed that the synapses related to these memories were locked, and that the painful emotions and the memories were forever linked. The resulting conclusion was that PTSD was incurable. The generally-held belief was that the best that psychotherapy could do would be to establish competing thoughts and memories a client could think about when the painful memory was stimulated. Many psychologists and psychiatrists believe this even today, and this is one of the reasons that Shapiro's original claims about EMDR were met with such skepticism.

Giving Mouse PTSD

Consider the following fantasy, and imagine the profound changes that could ultimately take place in the art of emotional healing

New Twists: Ideas and Terms that May Be Unfamiliar

if the fantasy were true. In this fantasy, a perfectly happy mouse is subjected to a laboratory experience that gives him a profound fear of hearing a bell ring. (Dear reader, please close your eyes if you are faint of heart and are particularly sensitive to witnessing emotional or physical abuse.) Each time he hears the bell, he is given an electrical shock, so that very soon he associates the sound of the bell with physical pain. Now, whenever he hears the bell, he becomes terrified, even if there is no electrical shock. (If you've closed your eyes, you can open them now; it gets better from here.) Next he is shown that the bell actually poses no real threat. This would be akin to cognitive behavioral therapy, if the mouse could understand language. "See, it can't hurt you. It's just a bell." The difference is that, unlike cognitive therapy, that simple logic is accompanied by ringing the bell, stimulating the associated emotion.

Establishing the Lack of Real Danger

Now the mouse can see that there is in fact no real danger. The bell is rung, and he still becomes terrified, but this makes no sense to him. He's afraid of a bell. This is an irrational fear. He is reminded of the events that occurred that caused him to be afraid. During those events, there was a real threat to him. Now, suppose we are able to give this mouse a drug that would obliterate whatever memory he is thinking about at the time the drug is administered. We make sure he is thinking of the original traumatic event when we administer the drug by simultaneously ringing the bell, causing him to shake in fear.

Erasing the Event in Working Memory

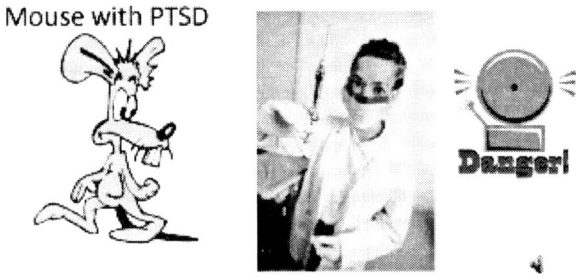

Suppose in this fantasy we are creating, something magical occurs; not only does this drug eliminate the mouse's working memory currently holding the memory of being shocked, but all linkages between the original memory of being shocked and the powerful fear that resulted are extinguished.

MOUSE Without PTSD

Now our hero can relax and return to his happy life. The bell can ring now and he doesn't even notice. The linkage between the memory and the powerful emotion is broken. Is this a wild futuristic fantasy? Might it be someday possible to apply Electroconvulsive Therapy (ECT), rather than a memory erasing drug, to human beings while stimulating the memory of a traumatic event; might this break the link between the memory and the powerful negative emotions? In fact, the scenario just described with the mouse has been demonstrated with a variety of animal subjects, and ECT has been applied in this selective way producing impressive results : (Misanin, J. R., Miller, R. R., & Lewis , D. J. 1968; Rubin, R. D. ,1976; Rubin, R. D., Fried, R., & Franks, C. M. (1969).). Although not identical, the bilateral stimulation that is applied in EMDR is analogous to the injection given the mouse, and the end result is that traumatic affect becomes unlinked from its associated memory.

What would happen if we gave the injection to the mouse without simultaneously ringing the bell? Obviously, to achieve this amazing healing, we must bring the traumatic event into working memory by ringing the bell. The same is true when conducting EMDR. **To resolve a traumatic memory, it is necessary to ring the bell,** and we do this in the Assessment Phase (Phase III).

But it turns out that ringing the bell is not enough. Recent research has confirmed what we as EMDR clinicians already knew: despite fifty years of research conclusions to the contrary, trauma memories can be extinguished. The importance of this recent research and its implications for the practice of psychotherapy cannot be overstated. But scientists have gone further than establishing simply that trauma memories can be extinguished, identifying exactly what two conditions must be met for a locked trauma memory to become unlocked, making it vulnerable to change. According to neuroscientific research, the presence of these two conditions will open an approximately five hour window in which the activated memory becomes plastic, and subject to change ("unlocked"). (Pedreira, M. E., Pérez-Cuesta, L. M., & Maldonado, H. ,2002; Walker, Brakefield, Hobson, & Stickgold, 2003). This additional information is very important to us as EMDR clinicians.

To become unlocked, an emotion-linked memory must be accessed along with the accompanying emotion, and then new information must be accepted that is a mismatch to what is expected and predicted based upon the reactivated memory. The mismatch calls into question the original associated belief or expectations. (Duvarci, S., Mamou, C.S. & Nadar, K., 2006; Pedreira, M. E., Pérez-Cuesta, L. M., & Maldonado, H., 2004) Without this challenge, even if the memory is emotionally activated, it will not become unlocked. (Hernandez, P. J., & Kelley, A. E. ,2004; Mileusnic, R., Lancashire, C. L., & Rose, S. P. R. ,2005). In EMDR terminology, this means that the target must be activated, and the associated belief or expectation (negative cognition) must be successfully challenged with a contrary belief or observation (adaptive adult perspective) in order for the memory to become unlocked and available for resolution. If there are multiple negative cognitions, they must all be challenged in order for the memory to resolve. Dr. Lewis Engel has pointed out (personal conversation) that the mismatch might be created in EMDR simply by the unexpected experience of recalling the activated memory and simultaneously moving one's eyes. It would be fittingly ironic if the weird quality of EMDR that initially caused so much skepticism in academic circles might, in fact, be a central factor in what causes it to be effective.

The challenge to the original belief can take different forms: the client's spontaneous associations during the alternating bilateral stimulation (BLS); the felt sense of the validity of the positive cognition; or a cognitive interweave that causes an adaptive adult perspective to come into play contradicting the negative cognition. It should be noted that just "lighting up" a target, according to this research, is not enough to produce the conditions necessary for change, unless the negative cognition is successfully challenged. A common EMDR practice when a client comes into the session distraught is to begin bilateral stimulation before completing the assessment, in order to give the client some immediate relief. Based on the neuroscientific research I think it important, after these initial sets or once the disturbance level has subsided somewhat, to go back and ask the client about the negative and positive cognitions in order to be sure that the conditions necessary for change are present.

The Assessment phase of EMDR includes all the necessary ingredients for healing to occur spontaneously during BLS: the emotions and body sensations that light up the target; and the negative and positive cognitions that highlight the cognitive discrepancy between the irrational belief (formulated at the time of the trauma) and the present adaptive adult perspective. If the cognitive discrepancy does not resolve spontaneously during BLS, a cognitive interweave will act as a catalyst for the necessary recognition to occur. Using EMDR, we can now consciously ensure that these conditions are met. We are thereby able to resolve these memories that were previously thought to remain immutable forever.

Optimal Targets

These developments in neuroscience make it clear how important a well developed target is for successful trauma processing. In the transcripts in this book, I typically devote a third to a full half of the session to establishing a "crisp" target. By that I mean a target that involves an identified lighting rod moment with a clear affect-laden image, activated emotions, and appropriate cognitions, all of which are linked and mutually congruent:

- The emotion fits with the image, and the intensity is appropriate.
- Negative cognition and emotions are congruent.
- Negative and positive cognitions are about the present. (Listen for past tense and ensure that the cognitions are reformulated into present tense.)
- Positive and Negative cognitions are mutually congruent.
- Positive and Negative cognitions are consistent developmentally with the client's age at the time of the memory.
- Positive and Negative cognitions apply to presenting (triggering) event as well as earlier TARGET memory!
- Body sensations and emotions are congruent in location and intensity.
- SUDS level is congruent with description of the trauma, client's presentation, and words chosen to describe emotions.
- SUDS, NC and PC are all about the present, not the past, and are viscerally felt.

- The emotions and cognitions are consistent with the client's symptoms since the target event.

Floatback

Whether a clinician is looking for initial memories in clusters of like events, or following the "Three Pronged Protocol" described in Francine Shapiro's seminal text (1995, 2001), the ability to identify and revitalize the first instance of various clusters of memories is critical to being able to conduct successful EMDR treatment. In that book, to identify the original ("touchstone") event, Shapiro suggests asking the client, "When is the first time you remember feeling this way?" Later, in Appendix A of that book, she describes a "floatback" technique introduced by William Zangwill that uses the image, negative cognition, emotions and body sensations to "float back" to an earlier related memory. She also references the "somatic bridge" and the "affect bridge" developed by Watkins and Watkins.

I think the somatic bridge, which I will describe later, is a preferable way to begin looking for earlier memories, because it is based on physical sensation and bypasses the left brain. I think the emphasis in searching for the early event should be that the search is based on a right brain associative scanning process that is likely to be spontaneous, rather than a left brain scan that is more logical. Searches that are left brain, or language based, will only turn up memories that have words connected to them. Such memories are called "explicit memories." They have had narrative added to them. They are indexed in the brain through the hippocampus. And they can be searched in a direct way using words and based on the logic of their narrative. For instance, "Do you remember what color the shirt was that you purchased at the store yesterday?"

"Implicit memories" tend to be memory fragments, that are indexed through the amygdala and do not have words attached to them; they do not have a narrative, so a search based on a narrative is not likely to yield implicit memories. For instance, "Notice the feeling in your chest that you just described, and let your mind float back to an early memory" does not require logic or words to result in a relevant past memory. Most memories are implicit, so a word based search will miss many important past events.

Asking clients, "Has anything like this ever happened to you before" invites an intellectual process that often results in associations that are not really linked to the initial memory. For instance, if the client was mugged on the street by a man with a knife, and we ask "has anything like this ever happened before," or "does this remind you of an earlier event," the client can take that question in a variety of directions. The client can think "has anyone ever threatened me with a knife before," "have I ever been mugged before," "has anyone been angry at me before," or "have I been frightened before?" If the actual touchstone event was an instance of dad threatening mom with a knife, this kind of an intellectual search is unlikely to identify that event.

In my mind, "When is the first time you remember feeling this way?" is not much better. If the client is describing the same mugging incident and talks about feeling scared in a recent incident, asking about an earlier memory of feeling scared can result in dozens of associations to previous events, and is unlikely to zero in on the actual touchstone event. Although I have had some successes with the approach of using the image, negative cognition, emotions and body sensations described in Appendix A of Shapiro's book (1999, 2005) to "float back," I much prefer a simpler approach. (I like the term "floatback" and use it interchangeably to refer to a somatic bridge, an affect bridge, or a "float back," though they are technically not the same.) My problem with the floatback technique in Shapiro's book is that it is too complicated for the client. I think the client should have one simple thing to focus on; in my experience, having four things to keep track of becomes confusing and interferes with the spontaneity that is called for in the intervention. In addition, this approach lends itself to thinking and reasoning, especially for clients who tend towards intellectualization anyway.

On the other hand, the "somatic bridge" (Shapiro; 1999, 2005), asking the client to focus on the physical sensations related to a recent event and then instructing the client to let her mind float back to an *early* memory, produces a very focused search, and clients often respond with comments like, "I thought of something, but I doubt if it's what you're looking for." Although obvious to us, those clients might not know why the new memory is related to the initial event because The floatback is sensation oriented, and their left brains are not engaged. Note also that I refer to an "early" memory rather than an "earlier memory" so that the client can jump back to the actual early touchstone event and we do not end up stepping through repeated somatic bridges that gradually go further and further back in the client's life. Consultees who use the word "earlier" in the somatic bridge might report being unsuccessful at processing, because their somatic bridge yielded a memory from adolescence, when the touchstone event, the proper target, actually took place at five or six years old.

If you ask a client to think of something that's red you will be casting a very broad net. There are dark reds, light reds, bright reds and subdued reds. All of them will satisfy the criteria of such a broad search. The same is true for anger. If you ask a client to think of other memories involving anger, the client is likely to think of many events that are not related to the initial event. But the physical sensation specifically related to a recent event is unique. If we ask the client to focus on it and then ask her to let her mind float back to an early memory with a similar sensation, the search is more precise, and the resulting memory is likely to be directly related to the initial memory.

If this scan doesn't work, I recommend repeating the floatback (somatic bridge) to see if the failure was a result of the way the instruction was timed. Sometimes when the first two attempts have failed, I even repeat it a third time, and might finally get a good result. I also can follow up a failed somatic bridge with a floatback based on just the distortion in the client's sense of self (negative cognition). "Focus on the sense you have that if you ask for something, you are a

New Twists: Ideas and Terms that May Be Unfamiliar   11

bad person. Have you got that in mind? Good, now let your mind float back to an early memory." After that, if still no feeder memory has been identified, a therapist might try other kinds of searches that are right brain oriented. For instance, if the client is connected to affect, a therapist can ask the client, "How old do you feel right now?" Then he can ask, "What situation or event do you think of when you think of that time of life?" I intentionally do not ask "What happened to you at that age?" because clients often feel pressured to think of the right memory. I might even make the question as general as "Good, think of a child of that age in a situation." Keep in mind that even if the somatic bridge or floatback is not successful, it can still plant a seed, having the effect of making the client more alert to spontaneous associations to earlier memories that might arise during trauma processing.

The steps to a right brain-based floatback are relatively simple. Have the client think of the recent event. Ask the client what feelings stand out when they think of that event. Ask what sensations go with that feeling. Ask if the client can feel those sensations now. And finally, assuming the client acknowledges feeling them now, ask the client to let her mind float back to an early memory.

Once a potential touchstone event is identified using the float back process, it is important to verify that this event is, in fact, a feeder for the initial memory. It is not uncommon for a client to float back to an earlier memory simply because the therapist has asked her to do that, but the earlier memory she reports is not a feeder to the recent memory. The feeder memory should of course involve the same sensations as the original event. In addition, it should involve similar emotions, similar distortions about the self and the disturbance level should be at least as high as the original memory. The exception of course is when the client underreports the disturbance level of the earlier memory. This can happen for a variety of reasons, an important one being that the disturbance level may be so high that it would be overwhelming for the client if the memory were fully accessed. Clients can also underreport disturbance for a number of other reasons: they are not fully accessing the memory; they believe that they shouldn't have such strong feelings about the memory; they are not in touch with themselves; or they are intellectualizing the trauma, thinking it should not be very disturbing because they worked on it in a previous therapy or the perpetrator has since changed for the better. Sometimes, even if the early memory identified by the floatback is not directly related to the original one, it could be a good target in its own right for a future session. If so, I note that to the client, write it down in front of the client, and say I think it is important and we will be returning to it at another time. If the memory that results from the floatback is not truly a feeder, the therapist should usually direct the client back to the original memory.

xxxxxxxxxxxxxxxxxxxxxxxxxxxxxxxxxxxxxxxxxx

Adaptive Information Processing Model

The Adaptive Information Processing (AIP) model is the theoretical foundation of EMDR. Originally termed "Accelerated Information Processing Model," it offers an explanation of how EMDR might work neurologically. The basic description is that a traumatic memory is stored neurologically in a "neural network" relatively separate from the rest of the integrated memory networks (the "large information system"). In other words, there are relatively few associative connections between the "isolated neural network" representing the trauma and the rest of the system. The goal of EMDR is to lay down new neural pathways to connect the isolated neural network to the larger informational system so that the two neural systems become integrated and there is a free flow of adaptive information between the two.

When I talk about the AIP model, I often embellish with my own interpretation adding some drama to the model and offering an explanation in lay terms. I explain that the advantage of holding a memory such as a major trauma separate from the larger information system is that people don't tend to think often of these experiences. (In fact, they actively avoid thinking of them.) I go on to explain that, according to this model, these isolated memories are like neurological islands that have little or no commerce or even connection with the mainland and therefore stay frozen in time; they are not islands of the quaint Martha's Vineyard variety, with its horse-drawn buggies, but more the Jurassic Park variety. The advantage of the lack of links to the mainland is that the unsuspecting traveler is unlikely to accidentally make a wrong turn and find itself being chased by a Tyrannosaurus Rex. The disadvantage is that if one does by chance drop onto one of these islands, there is no immediate way to exit, so the experience is likely to be scary or otherwise painful. Once on the island, the traveler is thrown back in time as if in a time warp, and the world appears as if the passage of time had never occurred.

For instance, the middle-aged fireman, who as a seven-year-old was bullied on the school playground and did not fight back, may have come away from that experience believing he was a coward. In his seven-year-old reality, he believed that the only way to feel adequate was to stand up and fight and get his nose bloodied. Now, as an adult, when someone accidentally steps on his foot, he may be thrown back in time to the moment the bully stepped on his foot in the grammar school, and again chastise himself for not confronting the person who has offended him, restimulating his sense of himself as being a coward. Although fully an adult with a history of courageous acts in which he has repeatedly saved people from burning buildings, when thrown back to that world, he again thinks in the black-and-white terms of the frightened and humiliated seven-year-old.

This model has been described, with less drama, in EMDR trainings since they were first given. However, if one asks EMDR clinicians whose EMDR training was not recent, how this model informs EMDR treatment, they are unlikely to have an answer. Few will even recognize the term "adaptive information processing." It is only recently that this model has been given the attention it deserves in EMDR trainings, so that clinicians can learn how to use it to inform clinical choices in their EMDR treatment.

According to this model, the isolated nature of the original memory prevents it from interfacing with new information and from evolving over time; its meaning fails to be transformed by subsequent adult experiences and perspectives. Most adults witnessing an event on a playground of the sort just described would feel empathy for the victim. An adult might very well be thinking, "I hope he doesn't try to fight back, or he's going to end up with a broken nose." The victim, however, now a grown man, again feels shame when recalling the experience; when triggered, he even thinks about current events through the mindset of a seven-year-old. It is virtual time travel. The mature perspective available to him when thinking as an adult about other life events is unavailable to him when recalling this childhood event. During EMDR processing, however, new tracks are laid down, and new links are made between the isolated island of memory and the mainland. Usually, the client makes these connections into the adult world spontaneously; sometimes, however, some help is required from the therapist in locating these resources.

In order to assist a client in laying down new connections to adaptive adult perspectives, the clinician must know where they are; the clinician needs a map of the territory on which the desired destinations are marked. The more prominent or powerful the adult resource memory, the more easily it can be found. For instance, if the client has been a supportive nurturing parent to his own son, his adaptive adult parent perspective will, in most cases, be readily available to him during the EMDR processing of this seven-year-old memory. When, as a parent, he accesses the memory of his childhood experience, he is likely to feel empathy for himself as a seven-year-old. The bilateral stimulation of EMDR seems to facilitate clients in accessing these wiser adult perspectives. This client might report that he is baffled at how he could have been so self-condemning all these years. Sometimes, the client does not spontaneously connect to an adaptive adult perspective. This happens particularly when the client's adult nurturing experiences have not been effective or full. In those cases, the therapist is likely to use the map obtained during history-taking of the client's healthy adult experiences to help the client make the necessary linkages. Neurobiology tells us that "neurons that fire together, wire together." (Commonly referred to as "Hebb's Law" after Donald Hebb). The more a client utilizes a particular combination of neural pathways, the more likely the client will utilize these pathways in the future; memories and perspectives that are revitalized through resourcing will then become increasingly more accessible to the client.

Use of the AIP Model in Formulating a Target

This model is very helpful in informing clinical choices. The first place the AIP model plays a role is in history-taking and case formulation. In taking a trauma-oriented history, we are interested in all the events that were experienced, witnessed, related by a third person, or imagined, that may have produced a distortion in the way the person views himself or the world. It helps the clinician to determine whether resource memories need to be revitalized, identified, or refreshed prior to EMDR processing. It also helps the therapist determine what techniques to use to maintain an adequate balance for the client between past focus and present. In particular, if the therapist knows what trauma is going to be processed, and the nature of the trauma, the he can make an informed guess about what resources the client will need to allow processing to proceed successfully. This enables the therapist to select a resource that will be useful for that particular target. (This subject is discussed in greater detail in Chapter One.) Based on this guess, the therapist can anticipate whether the necessary resource is available and sufficiently strong, or will need to be developed further.

"How Do You Feel Towards That Child?"

Direct EMDR trauma processing does not work easily in cases in which the client does not have a well-formed sense of an internal nurturing parent. The cases where it works most easily are the ones for which it was originally designed, clients with a history of one or more single incident traumas. More complex cases often require a more elaborate process. Doing live demonstrations in EMDR trainings has made me realize how integrated resourcing has become for me with case conceptualization and trauma processing. There is always a way to proceed. When I sit down in front of a room full of people with a demonstration client I first assess the client's readiness for direct trauma processing. I assess the client's needs and capacities, and decide what I think she is ready for. If I think she is not ready for direct trauma processing, I look at what she will need first to help her become ready, typically resourcing, education or stabilization. In each case, I attempt to offer the client only what she is prepared to handle.

One question I ask to evaluate a client's readiness to process a particular early trauma memory is how the adult client feels towards herself as a child. Of course, when a client thinks of an actual traumatic event, the client's view of the child experiencing the trauma will be distorted. It is this distortion that is captured in the "negative cognition" (Shapiro 1995 & 2001) included as part of the EMDR Assessment Phase. In evaluating the adult client's attitude toward her child self, I do not ask her to think of the traumatic memory, but of herself as a child at that age. I ask her to bring up an image of that child and to describe the visual details. The process of describing what the adult sees in the image helps to ground the client in her adult perspective. I also ask the adult client how she feels about scooping up and holding that child. If the adult bringing up this image cannot feel caring and compassion for the child, I do not expect EMDR processing of that memory to proceed smoothly because the adaptive adult perspective that will be a necessary part of the eventual resolution is not readily available to the client.

New Twists: Ideas and Terms that May Be Unfamiliar   17

In these situations, when I determine that a client is in need of a greater sense of caring and appreciation of her child self, I instead turn to "dyadic resourcing," the subject of my book with the same name, as a way to gain access to that internal caring adult perspective. I begin by exploring whether she has sufficient access to an internal model of a caring adult and, if so, whether that caring adult can maintain that caring stance when focusing on herself as a child. Some clients can identify with the caring adult part of themselves in relation to children in general, but become critical or judgmental when they think specifically of themselves as a child. The objective for the EMDR therapist is to help these clients feel towards themselves as they do towards other children. Those who can maintain that caring perspective towards themselves as children are relatively easy to work with.

Others have difficulty locating an internal model of themselves as a caring adult, and in fact, typically labor at identifying any caring adults. These clients are more challenging to work with. The dyadic resourcing process enables these clients to identify examples of caring adults, and to build them into powerful internalized caring adult selves who are able feel compassion and caring towards their own traumatized child selves. In short, dyadic resourcing enables these clients to provide their own internal support, making EMDR trauma processing possible for the internal traumatized child. With the help of cognitive interweaves built around this resource, EMDR processing enables the client's view of her child self, and by extension her entire self, to change from a defective, unlovable, worthless, weak, or bad person to a lovable, innocent, well-intentioned, good person.

While the book about Dyadic Resourcing is addressed towards those clients whose childhood experience does not provide them with easy access to healthy parenting models, the clients who are the demonstration subjects in *EMDR Up Close* are, for the most part, able to provide their own resourcing for their younger selves. They typically have enough of an early parenting foundation that they can provide their own compassionate adaptive adult perspective when processing early memories.

The use of the AIP model will be a guiding principle in all the sections of this volume. My earlier volume, *Dyadic Resourcing: Creating a Foundation for Processing Trauma (Manfield, 2010)*, illustrated how the AIP Model informs history and case conceptualization in Phase I, points to the resources that are likely to be necessary for a given target, and sheds light in Phase II (Preparation) on the types of resources that are likely to be useful. The present volume addresses Phases III through IV. During Phase III (Assessment/Target Development), the therapist must take all the disparate information collected about a target and organize it into a cohesive, focused whole, so that the whole memory becomes affectively alive ("activated"). Then, of course, during Phase IV (Desensitization and Reprocessing), the therapist must continually track the processing in the context of the AIP model to make sure that the process makes clinical sense and is progressing towards an adaptive resolution.

Low-Hanging Fruit

Another subject relatively new to EMDR trainings is an elaborate treatment of case conceptualization. In the early days of EMDR, this was not so necessary when the technique was primarily used to process single incident traumas. Now that the range of EMDR treatment is much broader, case conceptualization is necessary. When I teach EMDR, I encourage EMDR clinicians to begin with what I term "low-hanging fruit," as the first target they process with new EMDR clients. This is a target event like a simple loss or single incident trauma that can be expected to process successfully in a single session or perhaps two. This gives the client an initial experience of EMDR that is very positive, instills confidence in the EMDR process and in the therapist, helps the client become more adept at utilizing the

New Twists: Ideas and Terms that May Be Unfamiliar 19

alternating bilateral stimulation (BLS), and creates a positive expectation about future EMDR processing that makes the client more willing to access very painful memories for the purpose of EMDR processing. If the low-hanging fruit memory is not related to the presenting problem, I acknowledge to the client that in our first processing session we will not be working on the presenting problem, but instead we will be familiarizing the client with how EMDR works.

Even after hearing it explained several time, trainees are often confused about what kinds of memories constitute low-hanging fruit. The designation of low-hanging fruit is not particularly related to the initial disturbance level (SUDS). Instead, it is related to the likelihood of complications occurring during processing. For instance, if a memory has a feeder memory, it will not qualify as low-hanging fruit. The feeder memory itself might qualify as low-hanging fruit, depending on the age of the client that that memory relates to and how the client seems to be responding to the memory. Memories before the age of three tend to be preverbal and are usually not clearly recalled. In addition, young children are so vulnerable at early ages that an event occurring at a very early age tends to be particularly painful due to the child's lack of internal resources necessary to contain painful affect and self-soothe. Such early memories will not be low-hanging fruit. Similarly, memories which trigger the client to dissociate will be relatively difficult to process and will not be low-hanging fruit.

When it is difficult to find low-hanging fruit for a particular client, I recommend going through the following list with the client, and using the list to collect additional disturbing past memories. For each new memory cited, evaluate the relative ease of processing it:

Worst experience with father, mother, sib etc.
Relative the client disliked the most (& why)
Worst experience in school/playground
Worst birthday or other holiday (i.e.: Worst Christmas)
Worst day ever
Worst sexual experience/Have you or anyone you knew ever been molested?

Times you thought you might die
Times you were really scared, sad, angry, or ashamed
Worst experience involving drugs or alcohol consumed by you or anyone else
Worst illness, accident or injury
Worst/first relationship/breakup
Most embarrassing or shameful memory
Most disturbing book or movie
Worst experience with an animal
Losses (of people, animals, things, competitions)
Natural Disasters
Worst experience with a doctor or dentist

Resolution vs. Avoidance: How to Avoid Rescuing

According to the Adaptive Information Processing model, in order to resolve a trauma memory the neural network corresponding to it must become linked to adaptive adult perspectives in the rest of the information system. The concept of an adaptive adult perspective is intuitively clear. I like to say that trauma memories are often resolved with a head slap. The woman who was molested as a child, and believed it was somehow her fault, spontaneously recognizes during an EMDR session that she was just a child at the time, and the incident could not have been her fault. When this new perspective sinks in she will typically say to herself, "What could I have been thinking?" This new awareness is not rocket science; it's more like a head slap.

The recognition of these new adaptive adult perspectives is critical to the EMDR process. When clients tell me that they no longer feel disturbed about a memory, but I'm not sure I believe them entirely, I often ask, "What made it change?" I expect to hear one or more of the adaptive adult perspectives that occurred to the client during processing. If I don't, I wonder if resolution has really occurred. Sometimes clients avoid fully processing a memory by imagining themselves being removed from the painful situation, either by their adult self or by a *deus ex machina*. By *deus ex machina*, I mean bringing a new element into the situation that played no original role, but seems to magically resolve it. Examples could be a powerful ally that didn't originally exist, a protective screen or glass barrier, a helpless or tied up perpetrator that serves to remove the threat, danger, or humiliation in the situation.

Removing a child self from a painful situation or artificially muting it does not constitute resolution, because no connections are made to an adaptive adult perspective. Removing the child is more like a temporary anesthetic. As an EMDR clinician, I am always asking myself whether my client is connecting to an adaptive adult perspective, or is simply avoiding the pain. Of course, there are times when such an anesthetic is useful, as in closing down an incomplete session, as long as the therapist understands that the lack of disturbance does not indicate that the target is resolved.

In a consultation group once, I was told of a case involving a police officer who was bullied as a child. During the processing the therapist asked the client, "If you had been there as an adult, what would you have done to help that child?" The client said. "I would have knocked that bully on his butt." The disturbance level went down to zero immediately. In the next session, however, the client reported that the disturbance had come back. The consultee wanted to know what went wrong. I refer to what the client did as "calling in the cavalry." The cavalry rides to the rescue and rescues the client from the painful situation, but this does not constitute processing. This kind of intervention is commonly referred to as a "rescue." A better way for that therapist to have asked her question would have been, "If you had been there as an adult, what would you have done to help that child feel better about himself?" The question asked in this way is not likely to result in a rescue.

Cadence Comments

Cadence comments are one of the lost treasures of EMDR. When I facilitated at trainings in the early '90s, cadence comments were taught at all EMDR trainings. They were also present in all demonstration videos conducted by Francine Shapiro. As one watched the videos, one could hear her in the background saying "just notice," "good," "good." Somewhere along the way, however, they were dropped from the trainings. I'm not sure why, because I think they can be extremely helpful, and every EMDR practitioner should be familiar with them.

Although fairly simple, most practitioners require a break-in period before feeling comfortable with cadence comments. Once mastered, they become second nature, and a very effective tool. For those learning to use them, I recommend staying at first with the neutral ones like "just notice," "that's right," and "good." It is unclear whether the ones with more content are consistent with the Basic EMDR protocol and, if coming from an inexperienced EMDR therapist, are more likely to be experienced as intrusive.

I like to say that for me cadense comments are involuntary. When I sit down with a group during the training practicum and the client in the group is either emoting or suppressing emotions, the cadence comments simply pop out of my mouth. Over and over trainees say that hearing them was a turning point in the processing.

On the most basic level, cadence comments involve a few words repeated in a regular cadence without very much particular meaning. I normally begin with "Just notice what is coming up," and then continue with some combination of "Just notice," "That's right," "Right," "That's it," "Good." These comments are especially useful when there are subtle indications of client affect and should be continued during stronger affect to reinforce the dual-attention nature of the processing. Cadence comments are not an attempt to reinforce a desired behavior; they are delivered evenly in a regular cadence, and mostly without reference to what the client is doing during processing. They strengthen the dual-attention connection between the therapist and client, helping the client to feel safe and to be aware of what is coming up inside while maintaining a connection to the therapist; they connect the client's recalled self to the adult self during processing, especially during recall of powerful memories. They should be tailored to the needs of the client, and reflect the therapist's attunement to the client during processing.

Some Examples of Cadence Comments:
    Neutral:
        Just notice.
        Right – good – that's it.
        Just follow my finger.
        Keep breathing.
        You're okay. You're doing fine.
    Distancing/Grounding:
        It's old stuff. (It's just old baggage)
        It's history.
        It's just a memory.
        It's over now. It's all in the past.
        You're on the train.
        It's okay – you survived.
        You were just a child.
        You're not that child anymore.
    Safety:
        He can't hurt you now.
        It's okay – you survived.
        It's okay to open your heart (exercise care)
        It's over now. It's all in the past.
    Isolation, helplessness: (In some situations)
        You're not alone.
        I'm right here. (Exercise care)
        It's okay. I'm with you.

Eidetic Psychotherapy

Eidetic psychotherapy refers to a form of psychotherapy that uses deliberate manipulation of a client's mental images to bring about therapeutic change (Ahsen, 1973). A discussion of this technique is far beyond the scope of this volume, but I will describe one of its basic principles that I use often. In eidetic psychotherapy, the term "eidetic image" or simply "eidetic" refers to an image that has life to it, and can change. In addition to the visual aspect of it, it has a somatic component and a cognitive component. (Does that sound familiar?)

Asking a client to access a scene from her past usually results in the client attempting to recall the memory. In that process, the client is focused on the past, and the client's present activity is "trying to remember." The resulting data is the client's best approximation of objective reality. Reality is static. It does not change. Clients often complain that the memory is not clear enough or they may not be recalling it accurately.

When I ask a client to recall an event, I also tell them that I am not interested in historical accuracy. I want the client to be involved, not so much in recalling, but in seeing and feeling. If it's an image I am asking for, I tell them, "I'm interested in what is in your head now, because that is what is affecting you. So, I want you to simply look and tell me what you see. I don't need you to be historically accurate, but I want to know what you are seeing now as you look back, because what you see now is what affects you now. If you see your friend wearing a pink sweater and your friend never wore pink clothing, what's important is that now you are seeing pink." This permission to "get it wrong" provides relief for clients who think they should never make a mistake. It also focuses clients on their present experience, rather than putting the emphasis on getting the past right. Even clients who tend to avoid affect will be more likely to connect to affect when engaging in present observation, as opposed to recalling the past.

New Twists: Ideas and Terms that May Be Unfamiliar

Neuro-Linguistic Programming (NLP) Accessing Cues

NLP accessing cues are another relatively simple skill that, when added to EMDR, can make targeting and processing more effective. The basic concept is that when people access an image they tend to look up and to the left or up and to the right. Although the two directions have somewhat different meanings, the basic concept is that either of these two movements represents visual accessing. Often clients are not aware that they have just accessed an image, but when I say, "What did you just see?" they can recall or reconstruct what they saw. Sometimes I put my hand up to the location where their eyes were directed, when I ask "What did you just see?" and they immediately look at my hand and recall the experience of looking up in that direction. According to NLP accessing cues, looking down tends to indicate accessing of emotions or body sensations. This is also helpful information at times for the clinician.

Container Exercise

In at least one transcript in this book, I use a technique that I refer to as a "container exercise." It is designed to help clients collect the disturbing material that has been churned up during the session and set it aside so that it will not be disturbing between sessions. There are many versions of container exercises, all of which seem to accomplish the same thing. The one I use is a modified version of one developed by John Omaha, PhD (2004). In this exercise, the client imagines constructing a container in her head, directing all the disturbing material into the container and then sealing it, the idea being that the client can take out small amounts of disturbing material for processing at a later time. This exercise seems to be very effective, and I've had some clients come back the following week after doing this exercise and say that they have had the best week they can remember having in a long long time. Since I doubt whether we actually put a container in the clients' head, I think of this as an elaborate metaphor that conveys to the client that she has a choice about what she thinks about, and she does not need to think about disturbing material.

These are the basic steps of the container exercise that I use:

1. Imagine a strong container. It can be made of steel, oak, reinforced concrete or any other strong material you chose. (BLS)

2. Install a valve in the top and the bottom so that you can control what goes in and what comes out. (BLS)

3. Do steps to make the container an eidetic image. i.e. "Now I want you to bring up an image of the container and look at it and tell me what you see. ...." (BLS)

4. Now open the valve at the top and without thinking of the details, allow all of the negative material we have touched upon and even negative material that we haven't drift to the container and go in. Sometimes it's helpful to think of the negative material as a mist or cloud. (BLS)

5. So, what percentage of the negative material is in the container now?

6. If the client answers with a number less than 100, for instance 65, "Now Open the valve again, and allow the remaining 35% to go in." (BLS) Then, go back to step 5. If the client says, "All of it," then ask the client to close the valve.

Processing Preverbal Memories

There are a variety of methods currently in use to process preverbal memories with EMDR. The one I have been using successfully for many years is to process the preverbal event as a story. I encourage clients to talk to family members, look at photos and think about the character traits they remember of the people who were around them when they were young. Then the two of us speculate, based on that information, about what might have happened to the client at a very young age before her memories had become consolidated. I caution clients to think of this merely as a story that we are making up. Sometimes a client protests that she might be making the whole thing up, and I say, "Yes, that's what I'm asking you to do." The indication that this story actually approximates reasonably closely aspects of what actually did occur is the client becoming emotionally activated by the story. Then, we can process the story just like we would an actual memory; however, a story about such a young child usually requires a fair level of resourcing before trauma processing is attempted. All the questions in the Assessment Phase are exactly like those used in the case of an actual memory. For instance, "What image captures the worst part of that story?" "When you think of that image, what negative words or phrase come to mind *about you now*?" This is the same approach we use when we are targeting nightmares or other disturbing dreams. Just as we do not require that a dream correspond to the real world, neither do we require that this story correspond accurately to the real world. Nevertheless, when these "stories" are processed, clients tend to experience symptom relief, giving validity to the process.

Dissociation

Therapists familiar with dissociation and experienced in working with it can usually spot it very quickly when it appears. Others, who have heard it discussed but not seen it, often miss it when it appears. One of the videos in the video library that JFKU put together of my EMDR work (www.emdrclinicalvideos.com) is of a woman who is probably DDNOS (Dissociative Disorder, Not Otherwise Specified), if not DID (Dissociative Identity Disorder). In the video, she switches often and verbalizes conversations between alters or parts. Many people who have watched that video have told me that it was very helpful in that it was the first time they actually viewed someone being extremely dissociative.

Most experts in dissociation agree that EMDR should not be attempted when a client is in a dissociated state. Doing so can lead to loose associations, disconnect from emotions, difficulty staying focused on a target, and the appearance of equanimity or resolution when inside the client is quite emotional, unresolved and possibly unstable. Since EMDR tends to bring out dissociation when it is part of the client's emotional repertoire, it is important that EMDR clinicians be familiar with it and able to spot it. Similarly, it is important for EMDR practitioners to be able to recognize when meaningful processing is taking place, as opposed to the client's responses being unfocused or rote. Readers familiar and comfortable with dissociation might want to skip this section.

Some indications of possible dissociation:
    Eyes not tracking
    Regressed appearance
    Regressed language
    Present tense
    Client unresponsive
    Preverbal target
    Dissociative indication from Back of Head Scale (Knipe 2009a)

Ways to ground a client who is dissociating:
    Close target
    Resourcing
    Pillow toss
    Walk around
    Name 4 red things you see
    Count backwards from 100 by 3's

New Twists: Ideas and Terms that May Be Unfamiliar   29

> Factual questions: "What was the difference in ages between your sisters?"
> Look at your hands; tell me what you see. How big are they?

It is critically important for EMDR practitioners to be able to recognize when meaningful processing is taking place, as opposed to the client's responses being unfocused or rote. Just because the client is producing new material, it is not necessarily the case that the client is productively engaged in the EMDR process. If the therapist is unclear about the quality of the processing taking place, it is almost always useful to take the client back to the target memory. This can help the client refocus if she has lost focus, and also help the therapist assess the nature of the processing.

Is there productive processing happening?
> Do the associations make psychological sense?
> Is the client jumping between events? Is the new one a feeder?
> Is the client tracking effectively?
> Is the client focused?

Do reported emotions that are typically difficult for other people appear to be difficult for the client? (Is the client working?)

Is there change in the client's present state and awareness? Is it change that sounds like adaptive adult perspective?

Is there balance between target awareness and present awareness ("one foot in the past and one foot in the present")? Is the client dissociating?

Is there habituation to the BLS?

Is the client bringing up associations that don't really seem relevant?

In the chapters that follow, the techniques and phenomena described in this chapter will play out clinically in the verbatim transcripts of sessions. Even concepts or techniques that are already familiar to the reader may appear in an unfamiliar or fresh form.

Wherever an issue is mentioned that is discussed in greater detail in this chapter, I have so indicated in the transcript commentary so that these more extensive discussions do not need to be repeated redundantly each time the issue reappears. Having read this chapter, you should have sufficient background to understand the various allusions to these issues in the transcripts.

2

The Right Target Goes a Long Way

(Video #12 in JFKU site)

The following transcript is of a 23 minute session that goes unusually smoothly, with the client spontaneously saying all the things we would want our clients to say during successful EMDR trauma processing, so much so that my consultees who have viewed it have quipped that they thought I must have paid him off to say all the right things. It is important, however, to recognize that processing would not have gone well at all if the series of floatbacks had not resulted in a solid touchstone memory. It is a good example of how EMDR works when there is an effective and accurate floatback, and the client is sufficiently resourced to process the resulting early memory easily and quickly.

The session took place after a class exercise in which people were asked to think of a very recent memory that was mildly to moderately disturbing, and then were taken through a floatback process to enable them to identify an early feeder memory. The purpose of the exercise is to show students how just about every recent disturbing event has an earlier feeder memory, and to introduce the somatic bridge, a floatback process that relies solely on body sensations to identify an earlier feeder memory (see Chapter One). Of the few people for whom that exercise did not work, I asked for a volunteer to do it in front of the class. A male student in his late twenties volunteered. (23 minutes)

CL: I thought of an event actually right before I got here. I talked to my boss. I have a part-time job doing counseling on the side, and basically one of the clients - I had to call him (my boss) and tell him I'm not going to be able to come; I'm going to be at this training. And he told me that one of the clients complained about me, saying I wasn't around to see this client, so right away I got like "They're complaining about me." This huge fear came up. "Oh, no, now I'm leaving. I'm going to be in trouble."
PM: Okay. So, then I asked you to focus on the image. Were you able to do that?
CL: Yeah.
PM: And the image was ...
CL: Of my boss.
PM: Of your boss, and then I had you float back to an early memory, and nothing came up or something?
CL: Well, nothing came up at first,
PM: And then?
CL: And then I got compliant, and thought, "Let me think of a memory" and the memory that came up was going to Disneyland with my family, and what came up was a picture of when I went --Like I remember flying to California and being there, but I keep remembering a picture that I've seen of me crying with my older brother and like my family there. But I pretend like it wasn't emotionally charged. But that's the memory that came up. So we did this floatback, and it was going to Disneyland, and –

> It's not a good sign when a client decides to be "compliant." It usually means that the client is going through the motions and no real processing is going to occur. With this client, even more than others, it would be important to check if the floatback memory was really linked to the original memory from which the client floated back.

PM: I'm collecting myself here. Going to Disneyland, and you were crying. What was the disturbance? What were you crying about?
CL: I don't know.
PM: You don't know. Okay, and what was the emotion that you think was involved in that memory?
CL: That's the thing. Once I went to that memory, in my head, I'm like "Oh, I got dissociated. I didn't feel anything when I got to that memory."

> The other possibility is that the memory was not very charged. Therapists need to be alert to the possibility that a client will do a floatback compliantly, and the resulting memory identified is not especially disturbing.

PM: Right. Yeah. Okay, so, I'm assuming that the emotion was some kind of hurt. What I was saying is that the earlier memory lacks two things that we would be looking for. One is it sounds like it's a different emotion, because it's kind of dread and fear when you think you're in trouble, and the memory is more of being miserable, hurt, something. (Yeah) Possibly neglected. Who knows what those tears were about, but they don't sound the same. (Yeah) And also it's not disturbing for you now when you think of it so those are two reasons why we wouldn't use that earlier memory. So, let's start over with the image of your boss. (Okay) And tell me what comes up when you think of that image.
CL: When I think of that image, I see his face talking on the phone.
PM: And what's the expression on his face.
CL: Disapproval.
PM: And how do you see disapproval on his face? What do you see?
CL: Like, mad features on his face. He's not happy; he's talking really stern, and almost like talking down.
PM: Uh-huh, he's kind of above you.
CL: Yeah.
PM: And what do you feel in your body as you picture this?

Before doing a right-brain floatback, I want to identify the initial memory we are working with and then identify a body sensation that goes with it that I am going to use as the beginning point for the floatback.

CL: I feel tightness in my neck. I feel a lot of stuff right here.
PM: Around your jaw?
CL: Yeah. Like tightness.
PM: You can feel that now, the feeling in your neck and your jaw.

If the client has identified physical sensations but is not actually feeling them at the moment I initiate the floatback, it will not work. So, before beginning, I ask, "Are you feeling that now?"

CL: Yes.
PM: So just focus on that and let your mind float back to an early memory. What's coming up?
CL: My parents fighting.
PM: Right. And do you have a specific image?
CL: Yes.
PM: Okay, and it's disturbing; I can see that.
CL: Yes.
PM: And would you be willing to talk about it?
CL: Yes.
PM: Okay.
CL: My dad is like yelling at my mom, and just yelling at her, not giving her a chance to say anything. He's calling her "stupid," basically.
PM: Uh-huh. Yeah. Okay, so on a scale of 0 to 10, how disturbing is that memory?
CL: 8.

The question about SUDS comes, of course, much later in the Assessment Phase of EMDR, and I will eventually ask it in its proper order, but I also ask it many other times, including during

> history taking and whenever a memory is presented for consideration as a target. In the training practicum, I have had many trainees who have gone through a substantial portion of the Assessment Phase only to find out that the memory they thought they were going to process was either not disturbing, or the client was not sufficiently in touch with disturbance to be able to process it.

PM: 8, so it's up there. And how old are you in that memory?
CL: 7.
PM: You're about 7?
CL: Yes.
PM: And is that the first time that happened, or that happened often in your childhood?
CL: I can't recall. I'm guessing often.
PM: Well when you think about being 7 and you're seeing your parents fighting, do you remember feeling surprised that they would fight?

> If a memory is a touchstone memory, the sequence of events should not be familiar. There should be some surprise, or there is probably an earlier memory that is related.

CL: I wasn't surprised. I was just feeling scared.
PM: Scared.
CL: Yeah.
PM: So is your sense that it was a familiar kind of fear?
CL: Maybe. I can't recall. I can't feel whether I'm surprised or not Yeah. So maybe not I guess.
PM: Usually if you are surprised, part of the experience is "What's this?"
CL: Yeah.
PM: But that doesn't sound like that's part of that memory.
CL: No.

Floatback does not seem to be bringing success in identifying the touchstone memory, but it seems to have to do with an angry authority, probably male. The next strategy for finding an earlier memory without activating the left brain is to focus on the anger. Since the boss did not seem to be angry in the initial memory, I would assume the anger is coming from an earlier experience.

PM: Right, so was your father a scary guy?
CL: Yeah.

A frequent question I ask is "how do you know that?" I am not intending to challenge the veracity of what the client is saying, but I want to find out what information the client is accessing and how. Is it a visual memory, the memory of an angry or contemptuous voice, a memory linked to a scar from a beating or the pain from a broken bone that did not heal fully? If the client knows something to be true from his past, there should be at least one memory that is telling him what he knows.

PM: And you just had something come up that enabled you to answer that question, "yes."
CL: Yeah.
PM: So what was it that just came up?
CL: Kind of, him yelling at me.
PM: Okay, how old were you in that memory?
CL: It feels younger. I want to say 4. I can't remember, but that's...

ASSESSMENT PHASE (PHASE III)

IMAGE:

PM: And when you think about being approximately 4 year old, and him yelling at you, what is the image that comes up for you?
CL: The memory that came up for me was being outside, and him killing goats. Like, he was literally killing goats for us to eat.

PM: And you were 4.
CL: Yeah, it got me really scared and having to run inside.
PM: And that's also about an 8?

> I was guessing the disturbance level based on his apparent affect level, the evident distress on his face.

CL: Yeah! Yeah, maybe more. Yeah.
PM: Okay. If you like, we could actually process that right now. Would you like to do that?

> I felt confident that this was in fact a feeder memory for the one he started with. It came up very spontaneously and was specific. It was not an ongoing type of event, so I doubted if there was an even earlier feeder memory, but the real test would be whether resolving this memory also simultaneously resolved the original later one. Our contract for the demonstration was to identify the feeder memory, so I was asking permission to go beyond that plan and actually process the memory.

CL: Sure. Okay.
PM: So when you have that image of him killing - killing a particular goat, right?
CL: Yes
PM: How's he doing that?
CL: He's cutting its neck.

NEGATIVE AND POSITIVE COGNITIONS:

PM: Okay, so that's scary, and what's the negative thought that comes to mind about yourself now when you think of that memory?
CL: It doesn't make sense but it's like my fault. Like I don't know why I would think that but...

> I often say of a negative cognition that it should be something the client knows is NOT true, but it nevertheless feels true.

PM: So somehow it's my fault. I'm responsible.
CL: Yeah.
PM: Does that also mean "I'm bad?"
CL: Uh, yeah.
PM: Okay, and what would you prefer to believe about yourself when you think of this memory?
CL: That it wasn't my fault. That -
PM: I'm a good person.

> He had been doing fine here; there was no need to jump in and coach him. He had offered "It's my fault" and I had suggested that it might mean "I'm bad," because I didn't understand how he might think "It's my fault." If I were to do it over again, I would ask how it made sense. In fact, I think he was bringing up a different facet or channel of the target memory than I was suggesting. He felt he was bad, and he also felt it was somehow his fault.

CL: Yeah.
PM: So when you say "I'm bad," do you still have some resonance in your present life to that statement when you think of the memory?
CL: Yeah.
PM: Yeah, okay, good, and you'd like to believe "I'm a good person" when you think of the memory.
CL: And it's not so much "I'm bad" as "I'm not good enough."
PM: I'm not good enough.
CL: Yeah. I'm not good enough.
PM: So how does that relate to him killing the goat?
CL: I don't know. Uh-huh.
PM: But it's "I'm not good enough" or you somehow didn't do enough to prevent this from happening, right?

> After rejecting the negative cognition he was proposing of "It's my fault," because it didn't make sense to me, I am realizing that maybe it is part of the distortion. On the other hand he seemed solidly behind "I'm not good enough." But, I am still trying to make sense out of "It's not my fault."

CL: Or I couldn't stay out there and -
PM: Oh, it has to do with running away.
CL: Yeah.
PM: So it means, what, I'm weak? I'm a coward.
CL: Well, my brother stayed out there.
PM: Oh. Was your brother older or younger?
CL: Older.

> So, "I'm not good enough" has to do with not being as good as his older brother.

PM: Older, so you had to run inside and didn't do enough to prevent this from happening, right? You felt bad about yourself for not being able to handle this scene.

> I'm still trying to make sense out of "It's my fault" but leaning towards "I'm not good enough" as the primary distortion. Often there are multiple distortions that each show up in a different channel during processing. It is best to begin processing with the strongest negative cognition.

CL: Yeah.
PM: Okay, so now I'm always asking myself, does this set of cognitions relate to the experience with your boss? Certainly, this is a good target for us to be processing, but I'm wondering if that's what comes up with your boss, "I'm not good enough?"
CL: Yeah, yeah, yeah!

> A clear endorsement.

PM: Okay. Good. So on a scale of 1 to 7, 7 is completely true and 1 is completely false - what was the positive statement, "I'm a good person?" But, you said it's not so much that. It's more "I'm good enough". "I'm adequate."
CL: Yeah.

VOC:

PM: And when you think of that, how true does that statement feel on a gut level as you think of the memory?
CL: When I think of?
PM: Of the memory of him cutting the goat's throat, and you running inside.
CL: How true?
PM: How true does the statement feel, I'm adequate, I'm good enough? On a gut level, how true does it feel now?
CL: 2.

> I often ask the VOC question without the scale and then follow up by asking for a number on the scale, but, in this case, he already knew the scale and gave me the number.

EMOTIONS:

PM: 2? Okay, so the emotions now that are coming up, what might they be?
CL: Scared but sad.

SUDS:

PM: Scared and sad. And is it still an 8 or is it more disturbing now?
CL: It's less disturbing.
PM: Less disturbing. 0-10? 10 is the worst you can imagine. How disturbing is it for you now?
CL: 5

The Right Target Goes a Long Way 41

PM: So our talking about it has reduced the disturbance.
CL: Yes.

BODY SENSATION:

PM: Okay, so it's a 5, and where are you feeling that in your body now?
CL: My face and my stomach.
PM: Okay, good, so just focus on those sensations in your face and your stomach, the thought I'm not good enough, and the image. And the image is of him, your father cutting the goat's throat or does it have more to do with you running inside?
CL: Cutting the goat.

PHASE IV: DESENSITIZATION AND REPROCESSING

PM: Okay, so just focus on all that, and tell me when you have it, all those three things. The sensations -
CL: Okay.
PM: Do you have it?
CL: Yes.
PM: Good, so just follow the wand. <><> (Client becomes teary almost immediately after BLS is begun.) And just notice what's coming up. Just notice. That's right. That's good. Just notice. Good, good, that's right, good, good, good. That's right. That's right. Good. Now blank it out, and take a deep breath. What's coming up for you now? And when I say that I mean, it could be anything. It could be an image, memory, body sensation. It could be a feeling, a thought. It could be a change in intensity of any of those.

> The comments "just notice, good, good etc." are "Cadence comments." The are discussed at length in Chapter One.

CL: The memory that came up was of a dream I had where I'm laying down and my mother telling me, "It's okay."

PM: Uh-huh.
CL: It's okay. And, as that memory came up it kind of –
PM: helped?
CL: Yeah.

> When clients come up with positive associations very early on in the Desensitization and Reprocessing Phase, I am usually suspect. I evaluate to see if the client might be avoiding the intensity of the target memory. In this case, however, the client had tears running down his cheeks throughout most of the first set of BLS, so he didn't appear to be trying to avoid affect. It is probably more in the service of collecting internal resources to permit him to adaptively process the memory. Still, the positive association he made in the first set of BLS is very uncommon.

PM: Just think of that.
CL: Yeah.
PM: <><> Blank it out, and take a deep breath. And, what's coming up now?
CL: When it started, the intensity came up, but, as it kept coming, I couldn't hold onto the sensations in my face and my stomach. Like, I couldn't hold onto them.
PM: Couldn't hold onto them.
CL: Yeah.
PM: Uh-huh. So does that mean - can you feel them now?

> Again, during processing, the therapist needs to evaluate whether the disappearance of the physical sensations arose from dissociation, avoidance, or simple successful processing. There is no indication of avoidance or dissociation here. The client is saying he was trying to hold onto the sensations but couldn't, and he appears confused about that, wondering if he is somehow failing. Clients often ask if they are doing something wrong when they find themselves unable to hold onto a disturbing image or unable to bring it back up. I ask them, "For so many years, you've

The Right Target Goes a Long Way 43

been troubled by this image, and now you are having trouble bringing it to mind. Is that a good thing or a bad thing?"

CL: No.
PM: Okay. So when you think of the memory now, what stands out?
CL: It almost is like, that new memory kind of connected to that old one.
PM: The new memory being your mother in the dream?
CL: Because now when I think back, I think of running to my mom, and everything will be okay.

> This is a description of how Adaptive Information Processing theoretically works. The memories of the terrified child were originally linked in his mind to inadequacy and terror. Part of the resolution may have had to do with my reminding him that his brother was older, implying that it would be reasonable to expect the brother to be able to do things he couldn't. Then, the memory came up of being comforted by his mother, who was telling him everything would be okay, and not judging him at all. All this reinforced a new adult perspective that his reaction was normal, and that there was nothing to fear. Later, during installation, he will actually say, "It was normal for a kid." His incredibly rapid shift to this positive image leads me to ask myself if it was genuine, but it did feel genuine to me at the time. It has the quality of gratuitousness and spontaneity that makes it believable to me. I think if he were using a rational or methodical thought process to intentionally find a positive point of view to which he could escape, he would not have come up with this spontaneous-sounding association that is accompanied by tears and has the feel of childlike vulnerability.

PM: Okay, just think of that. <><> Blank it out, and take a deep breath. What's coming up now?
CL: I got dizzy from the...
PM: Is that right?

> I interrupted him again. I had been thinking that the processing was progressing beautifully, so I was surprised to hear that he was becoming dizzy. Dizziness often goes with dissociation.

CL: Yeah! What's coming up now? It almost feels like I'm watching the memory, because I was watching all that memory, but it's like watching it like from a third perspective.
PM: Yes.
CL: Yes. And I'm not there really - I'm not really there.
PM: Yes, it's like it's happening to somebody else?
CL: Yeah, and I'm just watching it play over and over.

> I did not take this as a dissociative phenomenon. The client was not moving off into other material, He had seemed to be comfortable with his affect, and there was no indication that the affect had ever become overwhelming. And he was actually replaying the memory over and over. This was probably a way of consolidating the mastery he was feeling over the trauma. Children, for example, will tell the story of a disturbing event repeatedly in order to master it.

PM: Just notice that. <><> And what's coming up now?
CL: It feels like it's farther away. It feels like a memory–even watching it is more of a distant–like I don't feel connected to the memory anymore.
PM: So, how disturbing is it now on a scale of 0 to 10?
CL: Like a 1.
PM: A 1. And what is the disturbing part now? What makes it a 1? On a scale of 0 to 10.
CL: 10 being really disturbing?
PM: 10 is the most disturbing you can imagine, and zero is not disturbing at all.
CL: Okay. The one is more the memory that it was disturbing than it being disturbing. Like I'm not feeling disturbed by it.

The Right Target Goes a Long Way

PM: You're not feeling disturbed in the present, but you know that in the past it was disturbing. It's just hard to connect to that now.
CL: Yeah.

His description matched my idea of what an actual zero is, so I took it as a zero. If he'd have given it a rating of 1, I would have asked about it to determine if something was still disturbing. If something was still disturbing, I would have gone on and processed it, but in this case I was convinced it was no longer disturbing. Sometimes clients have no disturbance but are reluctant to rate their disturbance level as a "0". They may feel it's impossible for something that bothered them all their lives to be gone. They may be afraid it will come back. They may feel it is boastful, etc. As long as I am satisfied that there is no longer any disturbance, I don't press clients to endorse that. I do, of course, check the SUDS for the present target memory at our next session.

INSTALLATION:

PM: And what about the statement, "I'm good enough?
CL: It doesn't feel connected to that. I don't think of that memory and think, "I'm good enough." Like - It doesn't seem relevant at this moment. No.
PM: Is there another statement that's more relevant?
CL: The thought that comes up is "I was just a kid." That's it. Like, I was just a kid. It was normal for a kid.

> The clarity and appropriateness of this positive cognition again confirms the authenticity of the processing that has taken place.

PM: Yeah Think of that. <><> What are you noticing now?
CL: I want to almost like protect that kid.
PM: You're feeling protective of the kid? Yeah, like "here, I can protect you."
PM: Just think of that. <><> What are you noticing now?
CL: An image of me holding the kid.

PM: Yeah. With your arm around the kid.
CL: Yeah, pulling him towards me and saying "It's okay."
PM: How does that feel?
CL: It feels powerful. Like, I'm strong. Here, I'll protect you.

> This is a good example of the spontaneous emergence of nurturing adult perspective. If it does not arise spontaneously when a client is stuck with a distortion in the area of responsibility, suggesting to the client that she imagine herself or another caring adult comforting the child can be a powerful cognitive interweave.

PM: Uh-huh. Just think of all that. What are you noticing now?
CL: Like a relief. Like, really empowering.
PM: It's empowering to take care of this kid?
CL: Like, that embracing movement comes in. Again, I just see like--

> All these positive connections that are being made during installation should be encouraged and reinforced with BLS. The time constraints of the training situation were probably what caused me to cut that process short.

PM: And you mentioned that the feeling around your jaw and your stomach had dissipated. Is that still the case?
CL: I feel a little tense here and right here (side of neck and next to left side of mouth). But it's not like pain. It's just I feel sensations there.
PM: Uh-huh. Is it good or bad?
CL: It's not bad. It's not bad.

BODY SCAN:

PM: No. So what I want you to do is close your eyes and just scan your body and tell me if you notice any disturbing sensation.
CL: Just in this area (jaw, chin).

PM: Uh-huh. So just focus on that. Open your eyes and focus on that. <><> What are you noticing now?
CL: It's like I can't hold onto those sensations. The sensation like leaves.
PM: It leaves?
CL: Yeah.
PM: And when you think about it now, when you focus on that area, does it come back?
CL: It's like lightly there.
PM: It left and it came back.
CL: There are sensations but it's not how it felt earlier.
PM: Not as disturbing.
CL: Yeah. A little bit disturbing? Not really disturbing.
PM: Not disturbing.
CL: Almost comforting actually.
PM: Oh, interesting. Well just notice that. <><> And, what's coming up now?
CL: Kind of like a warm feeling. But even throughout my arms.
PM: Your arms.
CL: Yeah. Almost embracing that kid. That embracing warmth.
PM: So let me check now. You started with this incident with your boss. How disturbing is that now on a scale from 0 to 10?

> I try to always go back to the original incident or memory to see if the work we have just done has indeed resolved or partially resolved that event as well. If it has not had an impact on the original memory, the reason is most often that the floatback went back to a target that was not really a feeder for the initial memory.

CL: Not really disturbing.
PM: Not disturbing?
CL: Yeah.

CLOSURE:

PM: Okay, good. So, I think this is processed. It certainly seems like it. But, if something comes up, we're going to do a practicum later in the day, and you can always focus back on it, although I don't expect anything to come up.
CL: Okay.
PM: And thank you for doing this.
CL: Thank you.
PM: Great demonstration.

3

Simple Processing With a Good Target

(Video #3 in JFKU site)

As with almost all the sessions in this collection, this session took place during an EMDR training. The beginning of the session is not on the video because the session happened spontaneously after the target memory had been identified. Participants were naming possible problem issues from their own lives or those of their clients, and the class was evaluating the relative difficulty of treating each issue. The client in the video said her symptom was that she has never been able to sleep in an empty house or apartment. She always needed at least one other person to be in the house. We talked about it and I did a float back with her. She identified a memory of falling asleep on the living room couch of her family home in childhood, and being awakened by a commotion that resulted from someone in the family spotting a peeping Tom at a window of their house. After floating back to this memory, the client thought this might be a good target, but declared in a challenging way that there was no way she was ever going to be comfortable sleeping in an empty house. So, the session arose out of this challenge, and was videotaped beginning at this point.

Several interesting cognitive interweaves helped lead to the session's success. The sticking point in the processing of the original incident had to do with the fact that bad things happened while she was asleep and not in control; she had woken up to a scary situation that had begun and progressed while she was sleeping and unaware. Two cognitive interweaves in the form of "providing information" were necessary for the client to recognize the cognitive distortions that had been introduced by her 8-year-old mind and had never been re-evaluated. Several months after that session she returned for the second part of the training, and reported that her symptoms had been completely absent since this session. (26 Minutes)

ASSESSMENT PHASE (Phase III)

IMAGE:

PM: Ok. Good. So we left off with the image of your father in his boxers with a weapon, although you're not sure what the weapon is. Is that right?
CL: Mm-hm. I could guess.
PM: But it was shocking to see that he had a weapon.
CL: Mm-hm.
PM: So as you bring up that image, even if there are unclear parts of it, you have the image.
CL: Mm-hm.
PM: Ok, so think of that image. And what's the negative thought that comes to mind about yourself now?
CL: Around that image?

NEGATIVE COGNITION:

PM: When you think of that image, what negative thought comes to mind about you now? Probably, "I can't protect myself."

> If the client is struggling at all, I feel free to make a suggestion about the content of the negative cognition. If it doesn't click with the client I will quickly drop it. Even if my suggestion is wrong it

will often give the client a clear idea of what i'm looking for. In this case, the suggestion of "I can't protect myself" comes from the presenting problem, her sense of vulnerability if she were to sleep somewhere where there were no other people. Normally, I might suggest a negative cognition if the client is struggling to find one, but in this case it was the opposite. I suggested this cognition because it was so self-evident, given the presenting problem. If it had not been so obvious, I would have offered her a menu of possibilities. In general, when trying to find a negative cognition of a touchstone memory, it is useful to keep in mind that it should be the same negative cognition that would apply to the original presenting incident or memory. Sometimes it is easier to work backwards from the recent memory, identifying the negative cognition that relates to it, and then applying that cognition, if applicable, to the touchstone memory.

CL: Mm-hm. I need protection.
PM: "I need someone else to protect me."
CL: Mm-hm.

POSITIVE COGNITION:

PM: That fits! And what would you prefer to believe about yourself? I know it might be way out there.
CL: I can protect myself.

VOC:

PM: Yes. And how true does that feel, on a gut level, when you think of that image?
CL: Like a three.
PM: Three. Oh, pretty true. And what are the emotions coming up now?

EMOTIONS:

CL: That I'm scared, that I don't know what's going on.
PM: We're not talking about then, we're talking about now.
CL: Oh, ok. Still scared.
PM: Scared. Fear comes up. Your heart starts beating faster?
CL: Mm-hm. Anxiety.
PM: Ok. Anything else?
CL: Tingling.
PM: Ok. Where?
CL: My fingers, my feet.
PM: Ok. Anything else?
CL: No.

SUDS:

PM: Ok. And on a scale of 0-10, how disturbing is it now?
CL: A seven.

BODY LOCATION:

PM: Ok. And where do you feel it in your body? I know you feel your heart accelerating, and you feel the tingling. Is there anything else?
CL: My throat.
PM: Throat.
CL: It's tight.
PM: Tight.
CL: Like I can't scream.
PM: Yes. Anything else?
CL: Still in my feet.

> Here we have a clear image, a negative and positive cognition that fit with that image, emotions that fit with both the image and the negative cognition, and body sensations that fit with the emotions. This assessment process has gone so smoothly, and the target is so

clearly delineated and internally congruent, that I am confident that it will process easily.

DESENSITIZATION AND REPROCESSING

PM: Feet. Ok, so I just want you to notice those physical sensations: your heart, your throat, the tingling, and the thought "I need someone else to protect me," and the image of your father in his boxer shorts with the weapon. Have you got all that?
CL: Yes.
PM: Okay, good, so just follow the ball. <><> Just notice what's coming up. Just notice. That's right. That's good. That's good. Just notice. That's right. That's right. Just notice. That's good. That's good. That's right. That's right. Just notice. That's good. That's good. Good. Good. Blank it out now, and take a deep breath. What's coming up now?

> I am using a wand with a ball on the end to direct the eye movements. The comments ("just notice" etc.) are "cadence comments," discussed at length in Chapter One.

CL: My ears hurt.

> This is an interesting association, especially as the client's association to the first set of eye movements. Particularly after the first set, I am trying to evaluate if the client is fully engaged in the trauma processing, so I pay particular attention to the client's response to the first set of eye movements. Generally, reporting of a new physical sensation is a good sign, especially if it makes psychological sense. In this case, I did not have a clue why her ears would begin to hurt when processing this memory.

PM: Uh-huh. Just notice that. <><> Blank it out, and take a deep breath. What's coming up now?
CL: Confusion.

> This association does make sense, because a child woken up by a lot of commotion would naturally be confused?

PM: Confusion. Just notice that. <><> Just notice. That's right. That's good. Just notice. Just notice. That's right. That's good. Good. Good. That's right. Good. Good. Good Blank it out, and take a deep breath.
CL: I feel frustrated.
PM: Frustrated.
CL: You're asking me to do two different things, and I can't.
PM: I'm asking you to do two different things and you can't?
CL: They are!
PM: They are?

> The confusion here arose from the client's immersion in the memory to the point that she is speaking as if she is experiencing the memory in present time. This indication of intense connection to the memory can be either a positive indicator for the likelihood of a successful outcome to the processing, or a negative one, depending upon the client's ability to also stay connected to present adult perspective. If the client is losing the ability to maintain an adult perspective, reprocessing is likely to be difficult. In this case the client seemed to have no trouble coming back to present awareness between sets, so I was not concerned.

CL: They're asking for details and I can't give it, because I was asleep.
PM: Oh, this is afterwards. Just think of that. <><> Just notice. That's right. That's good. Good. That's right. That's right. Just notice. That's good. That's good. That's good. Good. Just notice. That's right. That's good. That's good. That's right. That's right. That's good. Good. Good. Blank it out, and take a deep breath. What's coming up now?
CL: I remember the cop that came.
PM: Uh-huh.
CL: He looked like Santa.

Simple Processing With A Good Target 55

> This comment indicates that she is beginning to allow herself to consider positive associations to the original disturbing memory. Positive associations connected with the original trauma, such as a friendly policeman, a kind ambulance driver, a helpful family member, or a warm and competent emergency room physician, usually indicate that the processing is going well.

PM: Yeah. Think of that. <><> Just notice. That's right. That's good. That's right. That's good. Good. That's right. That's good. Good. Blank it out, and take a deep breath.
CL: Well I thought of all the other memories.
PM: Mm-hm.
CL: All the incidents.

> I was unclear what she was referring to by "All the incidents" and it might have been helpful to ask. The tradeoff, however, is that asking about "all the other incidents" might open the door to digression or an unknown amount of disturbance. It could begin a discussion that could interfere with the excellent start in processing that she has made. When I have a very clear sense that processing is going well I am willing to let things proceed even though I don't fully understand the client's associations. I think, in hindsight, she was referring to other images from the same incident.

PM: Yeah. Yeah. Just go ahead with that. <><> Just notice. That's right. That's good. That's right. Good. Good. Good. Blank it out, and take a deep breath.
CL: I'm just replaying the image and understanding it differently.
PM: Uh-huh.
CL: Why he was doing it?

> This is adaptive adult perspective; she is recognizing, as an adult, that her father was trying to protect her.

PM: Mm-hm. Think of that. <><> Blank it out, and take a deep breath.

CL: Calmness. Nothing else.
PM: Hmm?
CL: Nothing else.

> "Calmness. Nothing else." does not mean that processing is done. It might, as in this case, represent the end of a channel. It is necessary to actually check the SUDS to see if there is other disturbance.

PM: Nothing else. That's fine. So when you go back to the memory, how disturbing is it now on a scale of 0-10?
CL: Like a four.
PM: It's a four. And what stands out?
CL: The whole image of safety, and that's exactly what he was doing. What I picture as being safe.
PM: What you picture as being safe. (Client nods) Uh-huh. And that's why it's less than a seven.
CL: Because I'm understanding why he was doing what he was doing.

> As in this case, asking why something is a four can be interpreted by the client as asking why it came down from a seven. My purpose is to refocus her on what remains disturbing so that we can continue to process.

PM: Right. And why is it as much as a four?
CL: Because I still have that scared feeling.
PM: Stay with that. <><> Just notice. That's right. That's right. That's good. That's right. That's good. Good. That's right. That's right. Good. Good. Just notice. That's right. Right. Good. Good. That's right. Blank it out, and take a deep breath. What's coming up now?
CL: I remember sleeping in my parents' bed for like a year afterwards. Cause we were too scared to sleep in our rooms.
PM: Think of that. <><> Just notice. That's right. That's right. That's right. That's good. That's good. That's right. That's good. Good. Good. Blank it out, and take a deep breath. What's coming up now?

Simple Processing With A Good Target 57

CL: Nothing really.
PM: And when you think of the memory, how disturbing is it now?
CL: Like a two.
PM: Uh-huh. And what makes it a two. What's still disturbing?
CL: I don't know. I can't put my finger on it.
PM: Mm-hm. What are you thinking of right now?
CL: How you had asked earlier if I had never seen my dad in boxers, or is it disturbing seeing him with a weapon...which I've seen both before then.
PM: Oh
CL: So, I don't know. I'm trying to pick it apart.
PM: Well, let me take a guess. As I hear you talking about the memory, and I think of your present symptom, I'm realizing that the part of this that is still very disturbing for you is that all of this happened without your knowledge.

> I made this guess on the basis of something I think about throughout an EMDR session; how does this all relate to the original complaint. Since the original complaint was an inability to go to sleep without someone else there, I hypothesized that this client still believed that if she was sleeping she was vulnerable to danger.

CL: Yeah, out of my control.
PM: You were asleep.
CL: Mm-hm.
PM: So if you go to sleep you don't know what's going to happen now.

> This is a cognitive interweave in the form of providing needed information. The client was not aware that sleep represented a loss of control, which, because of the experience we were processing, she was equating to danger.

CL: Yes, things are out of my control.

PM: Think of that. <><> Just notice. That's right. That's right. Just notice. That's right. That's right. That's good. Good. Good. That's right. Just notice. That's right. Just notice. That's good. That's good. Good. Blank it out, and take a deep breath.
CL: I'm very anxious.
PM: You're feeling very anxious now? (Client nods) Just notice that. <><> Just notice. That's right. Just notice. Just notice. That's right. That's good. Good. That's right. Just notice. Good. Good. Blank it out now, and take a deep breath. What's coming up now?
CL: That I was replacing the fear with comfort - of the image.

   The comfort of the image of dad protecting her.

PM: Uh-huh. Think of that. <><> Just notice. That's right. That's good. Good. That's right. That's right. That's good. That's right. That's good. That's good. Good. What's coming up now?
CL: I think I just disconnected for a second.
PM: Uh-huh.
CL: 'Cause that memory didn't feel right.
PM: Huh?
CL: That memory of comfort with that image didn't feel right.
PM: Didn't feel right, no.
CL: So, as it being new, I feel like I disconnected, and couldn't follow for a second.
PM: Uh-huh. I was thinking about the distortion in this memory.
CL: Mm-hm.
PM: And I was also thinking about your comment that you had seen your father with a weapon before. There was a memory earlier of seeing your father with a weapon?

 It had occurred to me that the client may have had an earlier "feeder" memory that was making this one more disturbing, so I was checking. The client here makes clear that her father with a weapon was not related to a feeder memory, because it did not have a negative charge to it.

Simple Processing With A Good Target 59

CL: Not in a bad way.
PM: Oh ok.
CL: In good ways.
PM: So when I was thinking about the distortion, I realized that in your child mind, you felt like this guy could get you.
CL: Mm-hm.
PM: And there is sort of distortion about that he was locked outside the house.

> This is another informational cognitive interweave. The time left in the session is becoming short, and this cognitive interweave is used to accelerate the processing.

CL: I feel like he could get me. But thinking about it in my child mind that he could, but in my adult mind think no, he could not have.

> This is really the distinction we are looking for. The client is realizing that it is only in her child mind that she is not safe. This is the integration we talk about in the AIP model, the connection to adaptive adult perspective.

PM: Just think of that. <><> Just notice. That's right. That's good. Just notice. That's right. That's good. Just notice. That's right. That's right. Blank it out, and take a deep breath.
CL: I can feel my distortion leaving, my irrational thought leaving.
PM: Mm-hm. Think of that.
CL: Damn it. (Laughs)

> This exclamation is a reference to the client's earlier declaration that there was no way she was ever going to feel comfortable sleeping in an empty house. She is realizing that her issue is resolving.

PM: <><> Blank it out, and take a deep breath.

CL: I am safe. My dad was protecting me, and I've been protected ever since.
PM: Think of that <><> And, what's coming up now?
CL: Nothing.
PM: So go back to the memory. How disturbing is it now on a scale of 0 to 10?
CL: Like a zero.
PM: It's a zero, good. And what about the statement, "I can protect myself?" What was it?

INSTALLATION:

CL: Mm-hm. I can protect myself. I am safe.
PM: Uh-huh. How true does that feel?
CL: Like a six or a seven.
PM: So just think about the memory, in whatever form it's in now, and that statement.
CL: Mm-hm.
PM: And just hold them together. <><> Blank it out, and take a deep breath. What's coming up now?
CL: Nothing.

BODY SCAN:

PM: Ok. So close your eyes, and scan your body. Tell me if there's any disturbing sensation. (Client shakes her head "no.") Good. So, I'm happy for you.
CL: Thank you (laughs)
PM: (CLOSURE) And if over lunch, anything should come up, you can always focus on it in the practicum, although I don't expect anything to come up.
CL: Ok. Thank you.
PM: Good. Thank you.

Section II: Complexity in Targeting and Processing

4

Using Resourcing to Help Get to the Target

(Video #16 in JFKU site)

This demonstration session involved finding an activated target related to the presenting problem. The client was both emotional and highly intellectual, and finding the target was challenging, requiring 53 minutes, so that no trauma processing was actually done after the target was identified. The eventual key to bringing the target into focus was resourcing the client so that she could tolerate accessing the target memory. (53 minutes)

PM: Good so, tell me what you started with. What was that?
CL: I started with this week, not being able to…file a form that's needed to get filed for like a month.
PM: Mine's due tomorrow. (The date of the session was April 14) (Laugh)
CL: It's actually not taxes. It's something else, but yeah…
PM: Ok. This is called, projection. Okay, and - You seem emotional right now. What is it?
CL: Shame. Feelings of not being capable, not having a brain. Feeling like I can't, I'm not mentally capable. I know it goes back to I'm not

worthwhile, and loveable. So, all those things came up. It was very loaded.

As soon as I hear the presenting material, I am trying to make sense out of it, and I am thinking about what kind of target we are likely to end up with. "I'm not worthwhile" is a negative cognition or schema that is likely to have its origins from a very young time, perhaps one or two years old. Developmentally it refers to the person's basic lovability and entitlement to be in this world, and infants and babies get that from the loving attention of their caregivers. While Shapiro (1995, 2001) recommends "floating back" on the negative cognition that the client presents, I do not do that when I expect the source experiences to be preverbal. I do not expect a word-based search to float back to a source memory from a preverbal time. In my experience, preverbal memories can be processed, but I would not expect to identify one in that way.

PM: Ok, so -
CL: And I'm scared.

"Scared" does not go with "I'm worthless" so I assume it has to do with the present experience in front of the class.

PM: Scared. That has to do with being here?
CL: A little bit.
PM: Ok.
CL: Yeah.

It would have made sense to find out what else was making her scared when she said it had a "little bit" to do with the present situation.

PM: So, what happened when you floated back?
CL: I went to Kindergarten. And I'm blocking right now. Oh yeah. I'm blocking right now. Oh.
PM: Something about not being capable.

Using Resourcing to Help Get to the Target   65

CL: And not, um, mattering. Not being loved. Not mattering.

> I'm looking for consistency between resulting floatback memory and the original.

PM: So that, that doesn't quite (Client overlaps: "to my parents") feel like the same thing does it?
CL: It, it, it, there's a connection with parent, like my father and especially my father, and not being good enough. Not being... mattering...so I wasn't getting the kind of attention that my other siblings were getting.
PM: It's not an obvious connection to not being able to fill out the form.

> Consistency between feeder memory and original should be obvious. There should be no mental gymnastics necessary to see the parallel, so I assume we are going to need to find a different feeder memory.

CL: No.
PM: Ok. So we're going to go find something else. So, um, when you think-
CL: Inferior. Not having, not being - It's just something else that's wrong with me.
PM: Mm-hm. So, when you think of, "There's something wrong with me," you think of messages from your father. (She nods) But this particular recent incident has to do with this form that you don't feel like you handled competently -
CL: I'm incapable.
PM: Mm-hm. Okay.
CL: I'm no good.
PM: Ok. So, do you have an image that captures the upset with this form?
CL: Yeah, I have like this picture of this form with blanks in it, and it's kind of fuzzy around the sides.

PM: And when you picture that image...
CL: And I feel really stupid.
PM: Yeah. So, the picture of the form...Is that evocative for you? Do you bring up the picture and feel like...

> The snapshot we're looking for is an image that is evocative, brings up feeling.

CL: No, that's why I'm confused.
PM: Ok. So we're looking for another picture that captures this disturbance. So think about...
CL: I see it from a distance looking down on a view of myself as a little girl.

> This is not the image from filling out the form, but perhaps it represents a feeder memory.

PM: That's all right; you're doing a floatback yourself.
CL: Oh.
PM: Right?
CL: Ok.
PM: Uh-huh. What do you see?
CL: Um, it's really hard to see. Um, a very small person...not, um...being left behind or not left behind but not mattering, just, being, um, alone.

Again, this does not appear to be directly related to the original memory. It also is not really a snapshot. A snapshot must be a clear coherent picture. Much more is described by the client in this instance than could be inferred from a visual image, supporting my belief that she is not looking at an image in her mind. To encourage the client to look at a mental snapshot in a situation like this, I often ask, "What do you see that tells you that?"

PM: If I had a photo of this little girl being left alone, what would I see that would tell me all of that?
CL: (Exhale) Well, I have another image that also came up, which is an earlier image.

> When asked for specific information about the image the client is talking about, she jumps to another image. This suggests that there wasn't a clear image being accessed in the first place. She appeared to be describing more of a concept about herself than an image.

PM: Uh-huh.
CL: Which is being left in a crib.
PM: Uh-huh.
CL: And that image is...clearer. (Client is looking up and to the left, which indicates she is accessing an image.) Where I'm sort of standing up against the crib. Um...
PM: You're standing on the- holding the railing.
CL: And, um, I can't get out.
PM: Mm-hm.
CL: And no one's coming.

> Again, there is no obvious connection between the crib memory and the original memory. The client is jumping from one memory to the other, and there is no apparent coherent pattern related to the original memory. I decided to go back to the source, the original memory. This, to me, is a difficult clinical situation. Confronted with a situation like this, I question whether it will be possible to get the client to settle down and focus without additional preparation. I want her to be comfortable focusing on early disturbing memories and disturbing metaphorical material such as a story of what probably occurred when she was extremely young. This will not happen without sufficient resourcing. As described in Chapter One, in situations in which a preverbal experience is impacting a client, I process the "memory" by helping the client speculate from all the available

information about what may have happened to her as an infant or toddler. If that "story" is activating, we process it.

PM: Mm-hm. So let's go back to the form. So this went on for a month. And it's disturbing to you that you couldn't get this thing filled out. So, is there a particular moment that stands out as disturbing about this month long process of not being able to get this form filled out?

> I am trying to get a moment in time that will help to crystallize the nature of the disturbance related to this memory of having difficulty filling out the form.

CL: It stops me from moving forward in the rest of my life.
PM: Right, but I'm looking for a moment.
CL: A moment...God... I have fear of being yelled at. I have a fear of...um...God, one moment. I can't think of one moment.

> "I have fear of being yelled at," may be related to the target as well as to the current clinical situation in which she is having trouble giving me what I am looking for.

PM: Mm-hm. Well, how do you know? Let's start with when you first received the form. The first point at which you didn't fill it out.

> It can often be helpful in distilling a disturbing event so that it can be processed, to ask about the first moment that the incident began to become distressing. This is especially helpful in individual or couples therapy when a client partner is relating a story about a conflict with his or her partner. The first moment that they began to become upset is typically the point they were triggered. Floating back on the experience of being triggered will very often lead to a feeder memory from their childhood that is being replicated in the relationship. (Manfield, 2005) (Manfield, 2006)

CL: Okay.

Using Resourcing to Help Get to the Target 69

PM: So you can think about that, right?
CL: Okay. There are two things about it that, um, made it hard for me to do it, and I had to be perfect in doing it.
PM: Uh-huh, So, when did all that come up for you? "This is too hard, I have to be perfect."
CL: I just want to run away, and I want to run away right now. (Laughs)
PM: I want to run away right now. So what would you be running away from?

> The desire to run away does seem to relate to the current clinical situation, and her difficulty finding the memory that I am looking for. I am still trying to identify the nature of the disturbance, although "I have to be perfect" sounds like a very possible negative cognition.

CL: It, it's...(The client looks up and to her right, indicating visual accessing.)
PM: What's that image, right there?
CL: It feels too hard. The whole thing, the image
PM: Yes, and what was the image that came up? That one.

> Client is looking up and to the right. I am hoping she can get in touch with the image related to "I want to run away."

CL: I can't do it.
PM: Yes, and what do you see?
CL: I can't really see, but I have, like, dim shadow of people getting mad at me.
PM: For not doing this form?

> Apparently, people will get mad if she doesn't do things perfectly.

CL: Yeah, it's married to the other. It's married to...I'm feeling like this isn't inaccurate.

> Again, concern about doing it right, this time in the session.

PM: You know, I've already projected all over, so I might as well continue.
CL: Please do.
PM: So if it was me. Uh, it would be getting to that first question on the form that I don't know how to answer. And then, up comes my, my, feelings... about forms. Does that ring a bell?
CL: Well it's distasteful to have to do it.

> I take that as a polite way of saying that my suggestion was indeed projection, and for her it was off.

PM: Mm-hm. I'm looking for this worst moment. You had a whole month.
CL: Making a mistake, fear of making a mistake.

> "Fear of making a mistake" seems to be the uniting theme, but there is still really no target moment. I am trying to find a worst moment so that she can float back to a source (touchstone) memory.

PM: When did that come up? That fear.
CL: Well, this is such a theme in my life. In that moment, I don't remember. It was just one of the first... you know like, it's easy to fill out my name, it's easy to fill in my address, but all of a sudden, whatever the first decision I had to make was...
PM: Do you remember that first decision?

> I'm trying to help the client access a disturbing moment, rather than just talk about it in general.

CL: There was, there were many of them, there were several of them I couldn't make.

Using Resourcing to Help Get to the Target 71

PM: Yes.

CL: But there was, you know like...one, I think one major choice. Making a choice. And having to make a choice between something or another.

PM: And you couldn't do it.

> This appears to be a good candidate for a disturbing moment, but the client does not appear disturbed as she describes it, and she is referring to many such choices. When she first brought up this target, she got quite emotional, so there should be some particular experience that stands out and is responsible for the moment.

CL: Right! Exactly! Couldn't.

PM: What did you just feel, just now, when you said "right?"

> My perception was that there was some genuine affect at that moment and perhaps it will be a doorway into some disturbing affect. During this attempt to establish a target, I am continually watching the client's face and body language for indications that a thought or image is generating an emotional reaction

CL: Disgust with myself.

PM: Uh-huh. Was it a spike of feeling?

> It appeared to me that some affect had been stirred up, so I was checking that my perception was accurate.

CL: No. I mean, I'm controlling myself.

PM: Yes. But you may be feeling something also.

CL: Yes. Yeah.

PM: So, we're looking for something, yes?

CL: That I'm stupid.

PM: Yes, this is the thought you have about yourself. We're looking at a worst moment. The worst moment seems to be coming to that choice

that you had to make and "I can't do it." So that brings up feeling when you think of that moment, right?
CL: Yeah.
PM: And the feeling is?
CL: It's the pain of being in a frozen state.

> This was spoken with apparent affect. It may also relate to her experience in the session.

PM: Mm-hm, yeah.
CL: Like...
PM: Mm-hm
CL: Almost in perpetuity, not being able to move.
PM: Yeah. So...
CL: I'm not doing this...um
PM: You're not doing?
CL: I feel like I'm not coming out right.

> She is in fact referring to the session.

PM: The process? You're not doing it perfectly?
CL: Yeah, I don't have to worry because the process is what it is, right?
PM: No, but you should do it perfectly.
(Laughs)
CL: Exact, perfect. Ok, yes, ok.
PM: Ok, so, um...
CL: Exactly, I should do it perfectly.
PM: Right.
CL: Right, ok.
PM: We'll process that.
CL: Yeah, that it's not safe to make mistakes.
PM: After we finish processing this, we'll process THIS (gestures towards the class). (Laughs)

Using Resourcing to Help Get to the Target 73

> In hindsight, I think it might have been productive to shift gears and process her present need to do things right in the session in front of the class. It was already becoming pretty apparent that a solid processing session of an early related event was unlikely.

CL: I feel better, I do. That's good. Ok.

PM: So, um...So we have this moment of having to make this choice; not being able to make this choice; feeling this pain of feeling frozen, and that you're never going to be able to make this choice.

CL: Well, I can add that, what's coming up is "having to please others."

PM: Uh-huh.

CL: And it's not just pleasing myself.

PM: Yeah. So, think about that moment. Having to make that choice. Feeling...

CL: Should I not close my eyes, or close my eyes?

PM: You can.

> The issue of whether clients close their eyes comes up often in consultation. Shapiro has remarked on multiple occasions in EMDRIA conference plenaries that she does not think EMDR clinicians should allow clients to close their eyes during BLS, because, when they do, the therapist has a much more difficult time reading what seems to be happening internally for the client, and there is a much higher likelihood that the client could dissociate without the therapist noticing. Personally, I agree with her. I prefer to see a client's eyes, so that I can better attune to his or her experience. In the present case, however, there is no bilateral stimulation, and I want to help the client to focus, so I am okay with her closing her eyes.

CL: Ok.

PM: And see if you capture that moment in your mind. Can you capture that moment in your mind?

CL: I'm there. I'm warding off every emotion that I can ward off right now, but I'm there.
PM: You don't have to show us what you're feeling.

> I am guessing that she is afraid to show her strong emotions to me and the class, so I am letting her know that it is okay to feel them without necessarily showing them.

CL: Ok.
PM: Feel it. So, you're there, and what do you feel in your body? Now?

> Looking for a body sensation to facilitate a float-back.

CL: I'm very stiff.
PM: Where?
CL: Um, I'm holding all my muscles. I'm holding my gut right here.
PM: Ok.
CL: Um, my throat is lumpy, like I've got a lump in my throat.
PM: Mm-hm. Uh-huh.
CL: I've got like this - my brain hurts. I mean, like I've got this numb, weird place in my brain.
PM: Mm-hm. Yeah. Ok. So, um, is all that related to filling out the form, or some of it's related to sitting here, doing this in front of a class?
CL: It's related to having to face what I'm trying to face.
PM: Having to face…
CL: The issue.
PM: The issue of not being able to do what you need to do.

> This probably doesn't capture the issue that is most prominent now, which seems to be the need to be perfect, the fear of doing something wrong.

CL: Yes, yeah I don't like living with this.

Using Resourcing to Help Get to the Target   75

PM: Living with this, yes. And so, living with this says something about you. That you're...what? That you're what?
CL: (crying) That I'm incapable, I'm unworthy, I'm not worthwhile.
PM: Mm-hm. Ok. So-
CL: I'm not worth my, um...of father's attention, or my family's attention.
PM: So, right now we're just talking about this form.

> Client's comments are relevant but general. I would like to float back to a particular incident. It is becoming clear that the touchstone (original feeder) memory may not be accessible, either because it occurred too early in the client's life, or it is too painful (i.e., the client is too defended against re-experiencing it.)

CL: Ok.
PM: And we're talking about this moment of...It's a freeze moment, and a sense of helplessness. You can't do it, and you feel that in your gut. Yes? And in your...
CL: I'm not feeling the exact feeling of not being able to do it. Is that where I need to be?

> Client is indicating that "not being able to do it" is not really the issue, but she is also concerned about disappointing me by feeling something inconsistent with my expectations.

PM: Whatever is disturbing about it now, when you think of the moment of not being able to do it. What remains disturbing now?
CL: That I'm not good enough for my...um, to be loveable. To be...for my family to like me, you know?

> This is a clear statement of the theme of needing to be perfect (not make mistakes) because otherwise she will not be lovable. To process this theme, we now need to find an early memory related to this theme. "I need to be perfect" has a somewhat later feel to me than "I'm worthless."

PM: So when you think about, this is not um...
CL: How I make that choice determines whether or not...
PM: Whether or not you're loveable.
CL: Yeah.
PM: So there's a lot riding on the choice.
CL: Yeah, right.
PM: Right. So, um. So it has to do with feeling at risk. (She nods) Ok.
CL: Yeah, You can say that.
PM: And when you say that, what do you feel in your body?

> The overall strategy here is to get affect that is grounded in the body so that it will be possible to float back to an early feeder memory.

CL: I, um...tired.
PM: Where?
CL: In my body?
PM: When you say "I'm at risk." I said it. I said it, you agreed. What do you feel in your body when you repeat those words? "I'm at risk," and you think of the choice?
CL: There's an odd sense of, um...that I could, that I could die.
PM: Uh-huh.
CL: It's a very weird, sort of primitive kind of sense.
PM: Yeah, but physically. Physically what do you feel in your body?
CL: Not moving. Nothing wants to move. Not one cell. Nothing wants to have any motion in case...
PM: So...

> Therapist is again looking for a more specific physical sensation that will permit a float back to an early memory. By now it should be apparent that that is not going to happen, and another strategy should be adopted. Specifically, resourcing might make her feel safe enough to access the relevant material.

Using Resourcing to Help Get to the Target 77

CL: It's like I'm trying to stop physiological movement or anything like that.
PM: Oh, it's "I don't want to move." "It's dangerous to move."
CL: It's dangerous, yeah. I'm stopping myself physiologically.
PM: Yes, so how do you experience that?
CL: I don't know. It feels crazy.

> The client seems dysregulated at this point and not entirely present.

PM: Physically? At this moment?
CL: I'm not breathing.
PM: Have you noticed your chest is tight? Abdomen? Diaphragm?
CL: Yeah, definitely.
PM: Diaphragm.
CL: Right here.
PM: Diaphragm is tight.
CL: Yeah
PM: Any other physical sensations?
CL: I'm tight here.
PM: Your arms.
CL: I'm tight in all, in my musculature.
PM: Ok.
CL: My legs, I'm very tight in my pelvic region. My pelvic region.

> My experience in finding floatback memories is that an acute physical sensation that seems related to the disturbance works best. In this case the client is giving me a cluster of many different physical sensations, none of them acute, and most only vaguely related to the disturbance. I am doubting whether a float back at this time would be successful, but I haven't yet given up on the idea.

PM: Uh-huh. And these sensations are related to the struggle over this memory?

CL: This is…

PM: Yes?

CL: I just want to say, I feel…It seems ridiculous, as I'm being cognitive about it.

PM: It's not rational.

CL: Yeah.

PM: Yeah, we know that.

CL: Ok.

PM: So, but, um. When you think of having to make this choice, then you feel these sensations.

> Not yet having given up on the idea of doing a floatback, I am trying to establish that the client is presently feeling these sensations that are related to the original target.

CL: Yeah.

PM: You feel them now?

CL: Some are, yeah.

PM: Which ones do you feel now?

CL: I feel very - the bodily ones. I feel very tight in my -

PM: Abdomen

CL: Abdomen, and in my pelvis.

PM: Pelvis.

CL: I'm holding very tight.

PM: Arms and legs.

CL: Yeah.

PM: So just notice those sensations.

CL: Ok.

PM: You got them?

CL: Yes.

PM: You feeling them? Good. So now let your mind float back to an early memory. First thing that comes up.

> Although I did not expect this to be a successful floatback, it was the closest I had been able to come to identifying physical

sensations related to disturbance, so I thought it wouldn't hurt to try.

CL: It's bizarre, but I just feel like seeing myself as a baby.
PM: Uh-huh, So, that's not actually a memory, that's a concept.

When successful, floatbacks bring up disturbing memories with accompanying physical sensations, hopefully the same physical sensations that were the basis of the floatback. Concepts, or intellectualized constructed scenes do not have those same qualities.

CL: It's a concept.
PM: Ok, so are you feeling those sensations now?
CL: I'm loosening up.

I'm directing her back to the original disturbing experience to see if an actual floatback can be accomplished.

PM: Mm-hm. Ok. So go back to the choice that you felt you couldn't make. And notice what body sensations you feel now.
CL: I'm feeling this line up my leg. I'm still, I'm holding my pelvis not quite as much. I am holding in here.
PM: Mm-hm. So, that was the most definite thing you said. "I am holding in here." And you can feel that now.
CL: Yeah.
PM: And let your mind float back to an early memory. The first one.

Thinking these presently felt sensations might permit a float back. I tried to conduct one quickly before intellectualization would be possible.

CL: I see this blob, which I think is a baby.
PM: So, what do you feel when you see that baby?
CL: Sad.

PM: You feel sad. What do you feel physically?

> Client must feel essentially the same physical sensations for the memory resulting from the floatback to be a true feeder. In this case she does not.

CL: I'm, uh, I don't want to…I don't, I don't…I feel a little crazy. I feel a little bit…
PM: Physically?
CL: Mentally.
PM: Physically what do you feel?
CL: Physically what I feel. Abandoned, the feeling of…
PM: Physically.
CL: Not having…well, my skin sort of feels, tingly.
PM: So, what I'm getting from this is that, when you are trying to fill out the form, and you come to this choice that you can't make, that you basically shut down. You become helpless. And when you think back to the moment, uh, it reminds you of being a blob. Of being disorganized, unregulated, not able to function. Is that right?
CL: Yeah, that's accurate.
PM: Ok. Ok. And you feel ashamed about that?
CL: I feel a lot of shame.
PM: Shame. So, um, so this is a…
CL: I feel, ashamed.
PM: You feel it now?
CL: I feel ashamed now. I feel like something's wrong with me.
PM: Right. So you, it sounds like you have this overwhelming experience of helplessness, and, um, you feel shame about feeling that because you shut down. So it's an experience basically of…
CL: And it's not okay to have.
PM: Yeah, cause you're supposed to be able to function. So there's, um, the trauma that what's disturbing…By the way, 0-10. How disturbing was this recent…
CL: The recent one?
PM: Yeah, the form.

Using Resourcing to Help Get to the Target 81

CL: It's been at least, about a seven, I would say.

> Although I am asking SUDS out of its order in the Assessment Phase, I will ask it again when its time comes. For now, I am just trying to understand the nature and intensity of the various memories that are being described. Some clinicians would probably just begin doing BLS with the partial target that can be constructed from the intense feelings she felt when unable to fill out the form. Many such sessions are presented to me in consultation, and typically they are quite muddy. The client reports some partial reduction in SUDS. Sometimes the client actually reports a very low SUDS in order to please the therapist, but, in either case, it is unclear what if anything was processed. I try to avoid sessions like that, because they convey to the client a sense that EMDR is more hocus pocus than a precise treatment approach. Often, after a session like that, clients express an unwillingness to continue to do EMDR. They often feel hopeless about ever making real progress.

PM: What is it now?
CL: Well, I finally have gotten, made some decisions and so it's, it's not gone, it's I'd say about a four and a half, five, four and a half, five. It doesn't feel good.
PM: Mm-hm. Well, the disturbance isn't "I can't fill out the form," especially since you've filled it out. But the disturbance is the experience of overwhelm, and of basically falling apart and becoming disorganized, and just not being able to function as an adult.
CL: Yeah, that's right.
PM: And it reminds you of being an infant, who is disorganized, dysregulated, and can't do it, can't organize their world... Yes?
CL: Yes.
PM: And, that's a common or an uncommon experience for you?
CL: It's more common than I wish it were.
PM: How common are we talking about?

CL: I'd say it's common. Well, it affects a lot of decisions or activities that I have to accomplish.
PM: And you feel shame in all those cases?
CL: Yes I do.
PM: So the shame is of having so much on your plate and not being able to handle it, and you should be able to handle it?
CL: Yeah. And handle it to the degree that I think I need to, which is a high degree of perfection.
PM: Yeah, so. Let's just go beyond the age of three because, in Part One (of the EMDR Basic Training), we don't talk about anything before the age of three, so, um, think about after the age of three. Well let's do it this way. When you think of this feeling of shame and being disorganized and dysregulated and being a blob, what age do you feel now?

> This strategy for finding a touchstone memory is illustrated in many of the other transcripts in this book. It is an alternative to the Floatback, offering another way to bypass the Left Brain in searching for a suitable touchstone or feeder memory. The transcripts in this book were mostly chosen because the process for finding the right target was subtle and difficult. In practice, targets are generally easier to find than the examples in this book, and the Floatback technique is perfectly adequate.

CL: Five came up.
PM: Uh-huh. And so when you think of being five-
CL: Yeah.
PM: What do you think of? That one.

> I sometimes say "That one" in response to an expression on the client's face or an eye movement that suggests to me that a stressful image or thought has just occurred to her. (See "NLP accessing cues" in Chapter One.) Saying this often enables the client to become aware of a thought or memory that she had

Using Resourcing to Help Get to the Target

ignored, or that she had purposely not reported because she thought it was not relevant.

CL: My brother, um, who's older than me by a year and a half, two years almost. He's autistic.
PM: Mm-hm.
CL: And he needed a lot from my parents.
PM: Mm-hm. Why is that painful?
CL: Cause they weren't there for me. I wasn't, I wasn't seen. I felt like the more I did…
PM: You have an image now, you said "the more I did" and you have an image. What's that image?

> Again, I am responding to the client's cues, in this case an upward movement of the eyes indicating visual accessing. (See notes in chapter one on NLP accessing cues.)

CL: It's a general image; it's not a specific moment.
PM: Ok, so tell me what you see.
CL: Of my brother in need and my parents working with him in need and me not…
PM: Uh-huh, and what room are they in?

> I am trying to elicit a visual image. My sense is that her memories have been general, and getting the visual specifics can often bring it into sharper focus (no pun intended). Asking her to look at the image in her mind also forces her into the observer role, which helps her become more present and emotionally regulated.

CL: It didn't matter, it was the same. I'm there, but I'm not…
PM: So as you look now.

> Again, I'm trying to get a visual.

CL: Yeah.

PM: Tell me what you see. What room do you see? Just allow yourself to look and tell me what you see. It doesn't have to be a memory.

TRYING TO GET A VISUAL:

CL: Um, I'm in a room... In a house where, um, let's see, on Dover Street. Um, and it was a room where my younger brother was in a, in a crib.
PM: Mm-hm. Are you seeing all this or are you telling me a story?

> I'm trying to get a visual image, rather than a narrative.

CL: Well I'm telling you what I'm seeing. The image that I'm seeing right now. I'm facing this direction.
PM: Good.

> This is apparently now a description of what she is currently seeing.

CL: The crib is right here.
PM: Good.
CL: My little brother, my um, two parents...
PM: Good.
CL: And my other brother right here screaming...
PM: Yes, great.
CL: And I'm just standing right here.
PM: You don't see yourself? You're just there.
CL: What? What do you, what?
PM: Are you in the picture?
CL: Well, yeah I mean I'm in the picture. I'm standing right here.
PM: You are? So you're seeing it like a fly on the wall?
CL: Yeah.
PM: Ok.
CL: That's right.
PM: Ok. And you're seeing your back?

Using Resourcing to Help Get to the Target

CL: I'm, yeah. I see sort of the top of my head.
PM: Ah, I see. Ok. So now you seem to be calmer.

> Accessing the image has helped her to become more emotionally regulated.

CL: I hadn't noticed. But good, okay.
PM: Does that sound right?
CL: Okay. I mean I don't know if this is real or not, I'm just seeing this pic- image.
PM: Yeah, but it sounds like at this moment it's not a particularly disturbing image.
CL: Not this second.
PM: No.
CL: But. I didn't bring in…there's this piece of something, a story I know of. It isn't one. It's not a (particular) memory I've got, but I know this story that my autistic brother threw something that almost killed my little brother when he threw it into the crib. I never remember ever seeing that or doing it…or being there when it happened, but that's the story I know.
PM: Right. So, um, we're working with a sense of overwhelm.
CL: I feel crazy.
PM: Crazy?
CL: I feel crazy right now, a little crazy.
PM: Well, you're having a cascade of memories. So you kind of opened your mind and you're seeing all of these memories popping up. It's not clear what's related to what, but they're all related to "chaos" I guess.

> This chaos does seem to relate to the feeling of overwhelm she feels when confronted with the task of filling out the form.

CL: Wow.
PM: So, and what I'm trying to do is, to reel you in; to narrow down your focus. To get…

CL: That's always been very hard for me.

PM: Mm-hm. So, um, I'm trying to get you to connect to an experience that seems to be akin to the experience with the form. There's something about the form that (provokes) "I can't do it, but I'm supposed to be able to do it. It's overwhelming and my mind shuts down, and becomes disorganized." And that's shameful. And, you've had periodically experiences like that in your childhood. And so, I think probably the reason why we're having trouble coming up with a specific experience of that is because it's so painful. The feeling of overwhelm is one of the worst for a child because they lose their container, they just, they become incapacitated. Their mind loses its organization.

CL: Mm-hm.

PM: And um...

CL: That is how I feel. I mean I own that that used to be a very common feeling for me. Feeling like I can't organize.

PM: Yeah

CL: And it does feel like that when that paper comes to me - something like that comes to me where I have to get something accomplished...how to organize it, and then it becomes very hard.

> It is now becoming clear that the target being sought is too painful for the client to access it. The next strategy is to make that target more accessible by making it less painful. Since we don't yet have a target identified, more traditional methods of temporarily reducing the disturbance related to the target are not available. Instead, it can be done by building up the client's resources for the age period from which the touchstone event will probably be coming when it is located.

PM: Yeah. So, when you picture yourself at four years old, five years old- Can you picture yourself?

CL: Yeah.

PM: And what do you feel when you picture that four or five year old?

CL: Um, I feel sadness for her.

Using Resourcing to Help Get to the Target 87

PM: Do you feel disgusted?
CL: I used to, but I don't now.

> I am testing how much adult compassion the client has for her child self. This will shed light on whether the adult client can serve as a resource for herself, or whether instead more elaborate resourcing is necessary to develop an appropriate adaptive adult perspective.

PM: Do you feel compassion?
CL: I can't even think of, I mean I can't even wrap my brain around what compassion means right this second.
PM: Well, compassion means that you sort of want to scoop up that...
CL (speaking over him): No
PM: little child and comfort her...
CL (speaking over him): No
PM: And provide the structure she's missing.
CL: I don't, yeah.

> This response is an indication that more elaborate resourcing is likely to be necessary.

PM: Ok, so what do you feel towards her? Do you blame her?
CL: No, I don't blame her.
PM: So what keeps you from wanting to scoop her up?
CL: Shame and distance. Those are the things that are coming to me, shame and distance.
PM: I don't quite understand how that relates. You feel the shame, ashamed of her?
CL: I don't know. I don't know. I don't know. There's a distance, there's a...I don't want to move towards her.

> What the client is probably describing is that the child does not seem real to her adult self. The thought of the child does not engender feelings. In particular, she does not feel compassion.

Mostly, she would like to distance herself from the child's experience.

PM: You don't want to relate to her feelings.
CL: Right.
PM: Right. And, um...
CL: That's true. I don't want- I don't want to feel what she's feeling.
PM: And do you have children?

Resourcing tends to be easier when a client has had the experience of being a parent and has been nurturing, supportive and compassionate.

CL: No.
PM: And do you expect to have children?
(Client shakes her head "no.")
PM: You don't want to have children?

Without a parental experience to use to bring up an adaptive adult perspective, I begin to explore whether there is another child towards whom the client seems to have a compassionate adult point of view.

CL: I never wanted to have children.
PM: Okay. So, do you have nieces, nephews?
CL: No. There's one, step niece. But she's in a different country, and she's very distant, and we're not close.
PM: Are there any children that you feel connected to, like children of friends, uh?
CL: Not that are in my life.
PM: Well, that have been in your life.
CL: No. I made a periodic connection a couple of times with children of friends, but I don't have any children in my life.

Using Resourcing to Help Get to the Target

> The standard cognitive interweave, "If this were your niece or nephew ....," is unlikely to work for this client.

PM: And what about animals?
CL: Very much, animals have played a part in my life, yes.
PM: And, which ones?
CL: Poose Moose.
PM: What's that?
CL: Poose Moose. That was my most recent.
PM: And Poose Moose is a cat?
CL: She passed away in June, yeah. Yeah, cats mostly. Have played a...
PM: Ok. And, um, when you think of Poose Moose...
CL: And Magic Cat. (Smiles)
PM: Magic Cat?
CL: Yeah. And yeah, they have played an important...I can't even think of the word right now, what we were learning about today, um.
PM: Resource.
CL: Thank you, yes.
PM: Resources
CL: Thank you. Yes, they are my resources.
PM: Yeah, but also, I assume there were moments that you saw Poose Moose, or Magic Cat become dysregulated, panicky.

> The objective here is to stimulate a compassionate feeling towards a child (or in this case a cat) who is overwhelmed and feels helpless and dysregulated.

CL: Yeah, when it's been unsafe.
PM: Uh-huh. And what do you feel towards them?
CL: Terrible, terrible.
PM: Can you picture a time?
CL: Yes, screaming.
PM: Yes. And what do you want to do?
CL: I want the screaming to stop.

PM: Is that for you or for them?

> I am checking if her comment represents compassion.

CL: Well, it's for them, but I can see both.
PM: Mm-hm. So do you want to, take away their pain?
CL: What?
PM: Do you want to take away their pain?
CL: Of course. Yeah.
PM: So that, that action of sort of scooping them up is something that you'd like to do?
CL: I want to stop the other from...
PM: You want to protect them.
CL: I want to stop the person that's causing it.
PM: Yes, you want to protect them.
CL: I want to protect.
PM: Intervene.
CL: I want to intervene.
PM: Yes. But then, assuming that the danger has passed, they're still dysregulated, right?
CL: So I'm remembering now my dad being angry at my brother, who's autistic, and he couldn't help himself.

> This spontaneous memory arises probably because the client now has some compassion for her dysregulated self, so accessing the memory is safer and less painful. Notice what a different quality this memory has. It is a clear memory with clear emotions that are related to the original disturbing experience with the forms.

PM: Yes, and how old is your brother in that image?
CL: Maybe six, seven.
PM: Mm-hm. Yeah, and how do you feel towards your brother?
CL: At the time, or now?
PM: Right now.
CL: I love my brother.

PM: Mm-hm. And when you think of that moment, of your father being angry at him...
CL: I have a headache right now, I'm just telling you. Ok, what?
PM: When you think of that moment of your father being angry at your brother...
CL: Yeah.
PM: What, uh, if you could help your brother, what would you do now as an adult, if you were there?
CL: I would intervene; I want to stop my father from hurting my brother.

> This type if answer is common to this question, but it represents a rescue. The pain is ameliorated by taking the brother away from the perpetrator, in this case the father. What we are looking for, however, is an adaptive adult perspective, that leads to resolution of the traumatic memory. The next step is to rephrase the question in a way that prevents a rescue.

PM: Ok. And if you were there as a kind of a spirit where you couldn't actually change the action, how would you help your brother?
CL: What, wait, I'm confused. You mean the...
PM: If you as an adult were there then, as a kind of a spirit, where you can't quite...
CL: I would've compassionately pulled my father aside and stopped him, and, um, at the same time, you know, hugged my brother and told him it was okay, and he was going to be safe.
PM: Mm-hm. What just came up for you now?
CL: The ability to intervene as an adult is very different from that of a child, being there as a child- What? Did you see something different?
PM: Well, I'm wanting you to think of being there as an adult, but not an adult who can take action and change the script. I mean, Dad's screaming. You can't stop that, but you have an adult perspective.

> The objective here is to help the client connect with an adaptive adult perspective that will come from seeing the situation through

a caring adult's eyes. This is really a cognitive interweave being introduced before the target is processed with BLS. The target is already quite activated for the client, which is what made me consider using the cognitive interweave. While it will not obviate the need for EMDR trauma processing, it is likely to make the memory less disturbing. In fact, at follow up, the client reported that the memory was considerably less disturbing after this session. There was no information given about whether the session had had any impact on the original presenting issue.

CL: Adult, yeah.
PM: And you certainly don't blame your brother.
CL: No.
PM: You feel compassion towards your brother?
CL: Well, I do now.
PM: Yes.
CL: I was also angry then.
PM: Yeah, but we're talking about you now as an adult.
CL: Ok.
PM: Yeah.
CL: Right. Ok. Go ahead.
PM: So, you now think of it, and you can feel compassion for your brother?
CL: Absolutely. Yeah.
PM: Yes, and you would like to comfort him, in at least a kind of psychic sort of way, let him know that he's ok.
CL: Mm-hm.
PM: That this is not about him. That he didn't do anything wrong.
CL: Yeah-well yeah. I've done that.
PM: Mm-hm.
CL: A part of me doesn't want to.
PM: Doesn't want to?
CL: To comfort him.
PM: Because? Is this "you" the adult or "you" the child?

> This is a question I ask often. Clients commonly get confused about whose point of view they are expressing, their own adult point of view or that of the child. They lose their adult identity and become identified with the child. For EMDR we want them to be balanced between their child identity and their adult identity.

CL: Uh, the child.
PM: The child doesn't want to comfort him, but as an adult, when you look at him, do you feel compassion?
CL: Yes.
PM: And you want to comfort him.
CL: Yes.
PM: Okay. So, I am imagining that he probably, at that moment, feels something very similar to what you felt with the form, a feeling of overwhelm. "There's nothing I can do." And somehow there's a loss of love involved.
CL: I don't know why, but anger is coming out.
PM: Ok. Anger at me?
CL: Maybe. (Laughs) Yes.

> I had a sense that it was about me. I wasn't sure why, but I thought it had to do with my being responsible for guiding her into painful material.

PM: Ok. (Laughs) Can you feel compassion for me?

CL: (laughs) Oh God. I was very angry at my brother during those years, growing up too…
PM: Yes, yes. We need to differentiate between what you felt as a child, and what you feel as an adult.
CL: Ok.
PM: So as an adult, you have the capacity to relate to your brother in a compassionate way, and to feel for him, and it's not as overwhelming as the experience you would've had as a child, which was chaotic and overwhelming, and unbearable.

CL: Yes.

PM: And so as a child, there's a part of you that blames him for all of your pain.

CL: Yes.

PM: And so we really want to...

CL: And feels really guilty about it.

PM: Sure, you're not allowed to feel that. But as an adult, you have the ability to feel that compassion, and we want to keep those parts sort of separate, because it's the adult that the healing will come from. Because that's who you are now, and the child feelings are basically like the eight year old on the playground that someone steps on his toe and suddenly he's eight years old again. So, it's important to keep those separate.

> This is a reference to a description I include in the EMDR Basic Training of how an eight-year old who is bullied can come away thinking he is a coward because he didn't fight back. Then forty years later someone can accidentally steps on his toe and that memory becomes activated and he feels again like an eight-year old, and thinks like and eight-year old and wants to confront the offender to prove he is not a coward. (See Chapter One for details)

CL: Okay.

PM: So, as an adult, when you think back to your father yelling at your brother, how disturbing is that memory now?

CL: It's very disturbing.

PM: Eight?

CL: I'd say a ten.

PM: Ten. Well, um, I think that's going to be a really good target, and I think it will be a manageable target, but your therapist is going to need to keep reminding you that you're seeing this as an adult, because of the potential to go back to feeling like a child.

Using Resourcing to Help Get to the Target

> This target involves Dad yelling, which was coming up frequently but without a clear context in the original discussion of her upset around filling out the form, and it involves the sense of painful chaotic overwhelm that she feels when confronted with filling out the form. It is also from an age that is old enough that memory is consolidated and accessible to her, so that successful processing is very likely.

CL: Right.
PM: And feeling completely overwhelmed, and then being angry at your brother, and your father, and feeling discombobulated, and all that.
CL: I feel a lot safer and empowered, seeing it as an adult.
PM: Yes, of course.
CL: And holding the ten, holding the nine or ten.
PM: Yes, and my impression is that it's too much for "you" to be the child. But that you can manage it from the adult perspective.
CL: And that's kind of what the paper is. Filling out this stupid ass form.
PM: Oh, I forgot to ask you what you were angry about, at me.
CL: I'm not sure; I just know that I felt the anger.
PM: Are you feeling it now?
CL: No.
PM: Oh, okay.
CL: I was going to...Do you feel better now?
PM: Yes. Yes. The process worked! (Laughs)

> Our contract in doing this work was to take a recent upset and demonstrate finding the early feeder memory. Often in these types of demonstrations, if we find the earlier target relatively quickly, I offer to process the memory with the client, but this demonstration had taken nearly an hour just to identify the correct target. I have little doubt that this target would process smoothly, but, given the lack of time, I suggested closing the session down as an incomplete session. If you compare the chaotic nature of the

> original presentation related to this target, and the clear relatively simple target that we ended up with, you can see the importance of getting the target right before attempting to process it with BLS.

PM: So, um, we haven't even done any processing, but you're pretty activated. Less so, than ten minutes ago, but still activated. So, let's do a container.

> Using "container" exercise to close down a session in which the client remains activated. This is discussed in Chapter One of this volume.

CL: Okay.
PM: So can you picture a strong container?
CL: I've used containers of, of mason jars.
PM: Yeah, I'd like something...
CL: Something stronger?
PM: Stronger, and also, um, you can sort of construct it in your mind, and I'd like there to be a valve at the top, and a valve at the bottom so we can put things in, and we can take them out when we choose to. You can have it constructed of anything. I'd rather not glass, but glass will do it you have to.
CL: Okay. So I'm imagining now, that constructing containers, it doesn't feel good. I'm feeling like it's holding like, like, something that wants to, you know like gas coming out or something, that wants to, like you're saying release. And how do I construct a container that allows -
PM: Well, try making it bigger to release the pressure.
CL: Okay. Um...Is there anything that's like of the natural world that I can use?
PM: I don't know. What comes to mind?
CL: Well, someone once said they used, like a lake and they threw things
PM: Threw things out into the lake?

Using Resourcing to Help Get to the Target 97

CL: I don't like that because...
PM: I'd like to have something with a top and a bottom that actually can contain.
CL: Oh God. It feels tainted. It feels like nothing that something could handle. You know what I mean?
PM: Well that's the whole idea.
CL: Yeah. It feels like, uh, I don't want to pollute something. What?
PM: Did you see Ghostbusters? (a movie)
CL: I don't think so.
PM: No?
CL: I'm sorry (laughs).

(Male observer says "Different generation")

CL: (laughs) Oh God, what do people use?
PM: Oh, people make it out of concrete, or steel, or oak and they just construct it in their minds. Huge oak wine barrel.
CL: Well, oak is good. I like oak.
PM: Okay.
CL: Okay. Oak.
PM: Okay. So just imagine, imagine an oak container, really strong.
CL: Okay.
PM: And, uh, you might want to add some steel, wrapping to keep it really strong and imagine a valve at the top and a valve at the bottom.
CL: I see like an old fashioned tank house, because we used to have a tank house. Old fashioned oak.
PM: Mm-hm. Good.
CL: Alright, good.
PM: Okay, so imagine opening the valve at the top.
CL: Alright.
PM: And having all this stuff from your childhood, all the chaos, all the feelings...
CL: Okay.
PM: Imagine it all flowing into the valve, kind of like a black smoke, or a mist, or...

CL: Oh it's like, it's the dregs of a wine. It's like an old oak wine barrel.
PM: Yes.
CL: It's like the dregs of a really nasty...
PM: Uh-huh. Yeah. Well, just imagine it all going in.
CL: I can do that.
PM: Mm-hm. Just let it all go in. You don't have to think about the details of any particular piece.

> Sometimes clients attempt to think of each source of disturbance as they put it in the container, and the result is that they end up more activated when they are done, rather than less activated.

CL: Ok.
PM: So what percentage is in there now?
CL: Sixty.
PM: Sixty, good. And, and can you just think about the forty percent that's not in there.
CL: Ok.
PM: And, um, just follow the ball, and just imagine that forty percent going in. <><> And what percentage is in there now?
CL: Four. Four.
PM: Four percent is in there? Or four percent is out?
CL: There's, oh I'm sorry. There's only four percent left.
PM: Ok. Good. So can you picture the four percent?
CL: Yeah.
PM: Just imagine that going in. <><> Tell me when you've got as much in there, as is going to go.
CL: Ok, that's probably it, I think. I think that's pretty much it, as is going to go.
PM: Pretty much. Uh-huh. So what's that? What percentage is in there?
CL: Oh, like half a percent.
PM: Half a percent is out?
CL: Yeah. A half percent is out.

Using Resourcing to Help Get to the Target

PM: Uh-huh. So just, in your mind, just push that half percent into the...
CL: Ok. I just did it.
PM: (laughs) Ok. Now picture sealing...
CL: I did. I had to cork it.
PM: Put the cork in good. Do you need to kind of hit it with a mallet or something?
CL: Ok, I can do that. A little wax...
PM: Yeah, a little wax sounds good. Sounds good.

> I am always attempting to notice little gratuitous details, like in this case the wax, that a client offers when involved in any process that she is doing at my direction. By "gratuitous" I mean a detail that is extra, that represents the client's own original spontaneous contribution to the process. Those details seem to indicate that the client is involved in her own process and is not simply trying to comply and follow my instructions.

CL: Alright.
PM: Ok. Great. How do you feel?
CL: Um, my muscles aren't tight, like they were. I do have a little bit of tightness, but not as, I'm not...
PM: Not feeling terribly activated.
CL: Yeah
PM: Yeah. Think you're going to be able to go to lunch?
CL: I think I'm fine, thank you.
PM: Good, You're welcome. Thank you.

5 Month Follow-up:
A very important part of the session was when you put accurate words to my experience. As a young child I wouldn't have had those words to describe my experience: A feeling of overwhelm, the child loses her container and becomes incapacitated and the mind loses its capacity for organization. Ironically, as an adult, when my child memory is triggered, I still struggle at finding words to describe my experience. The thread connecting the freeze mode and cognitive disorganization I

enter when I have to figure out the right answer in adulthood, with what I experienced in childhood, feels accurate. Providing me with your accurate adult clinical interpretation was at least as important as following the thread and anchoring my resource. It lifted the sensation of feeling crazy.

I recall thinking after the session that we had done bilateral stimulation but, after reviewing the video of the session, I recognized that that was a bit of resource installation at the end. Still, the bit of BLS we did was an important part of the experience, leaving me feeling safer. So, bottom line: it was a real gift to me, to have you help me make sense of a very painful, incapacitating experience.

5

Floatback To Four Years Old

(Video #4 in JFKU site)

This session followed a class exercise in which people were to float back from a slightly to moderately disturbing event that had occurred in the past week

PM: So, what happened when we did the exercise?
CL: The recent memory that I had was I woke up one morning, and my husband was looking for his phone, which is an ongoing thing because he always looses stuff. He was in the bathroom and banging through his drawers in his closet, and I heard him muttering some curse words under his breath because he was looking for his phone. My instant response to this was kind of like the guy on the video last night. "It's my fault."
PM: Oh I see.
CL: Which is stupid because I was asleep.
PM: Right.
CL: And then when I floated back.
PM: Let me just ask you something.
CL: Okay.

PM: You look like you're a little activated just thinking of the event, is that right?
CL: It could be, or it could be because everyone is looking at me (laughs).
PM: Oh yeah, that's activating. Okay.

> As a rule, whenever I see any kind of activation in the client, I ask about it. Typically, that involves interrupting the client in mid sentence, because, if I wait for them to finish their thought, the affect may be long gone, especially if it is an uncomfortable affect that the client wants to defend against by throwing out a stream of verbiage. In this case, my impression was wrong, but there was no harm done in checking that out with the client.

CL: Everybody close your eyes now (laughs).
PM: Okay, so go ahead. I interrupted.
CL: Okay. When I floated back, and I don't know if this is what you're looking for, but I found a memory I have of being on my front porch. It was my first anniversary, with my first husband. And I was looking at the mostly dead flowerbed. It was married student housing in Texas. And I was thinking, "I've destroyed my life." But I don't know why I was thinking that. It's just a memory of being in that moment, and I don't know why. So I don't know if that's what you were looking for, but it didn't seem connected...
PM: Didn't seem connected, because the emotion was different, for one thing?
CL: The emotion felt the same.
PM: Oh.
CL: But I don't know why I was feeling it at that point in time, I guess.
PM: Ok, so the emotion was remorse?
CL: More fear I think.
PM: Fear. "I've destroyed my life."
CL: Like I'm stuck. I've made a decision that now I'm stuck with, and I think it was wrong.
PM: So, trapped.

CL: Yeah.
PM: And that fits with the experience of your husband looking for his cell phone?
CL: It was the same fear, yeah.
PM: So you felt fear.
CL: Fear. It was like here, in my throat.

> The connection between the memory with her first husband and her second didn't seem clear to me at this point. What was the fear that came up with her recent event? And, what would that have to do with feeling trapped? There, was some indication of affect in this moment.

PM: So I'm assuming it doesn't have to do with sitting in front of the class, because it's when you talk about it, that you become emotional. Is that right?
CL: Yeah I think so, because I wasn't even thinking about the class right then.
PM: Okay. So you feel it where in your body?
CL: Kind of all up through here, but really clenching here and here I think. (Client motions to her throat)
PM: Ok, so you get the connection between the two events, it's just you're not sure why you were feeling that in the early event. The emotions don't make sense.
CL: Yeah I can't remember anything around that moment, of why I was feeling that way.
PM: Right. So just stay with that feeling. Can you feel it now, the feeling in your chest and your throat?
CL: Mm-hm.
PM: Yes?
CL: Yeah.
PM: Now let your mind float back to an early memory. What's the first thing that came up?
CL: Another one I have no connection for.
PM: Uh-huh.

CL: I was in a carport, I must have been four or five, and we had a cage with squirrels in it. And I was just there looking at the cage. I don't really associate the feeling with that though. I don't know why I went there.

> For this memory to have been a feeder memory, it would need to have the same emotion connected to it. Since it is earlier than the memory with her first husband, it is preferable as a target if it is indeed a feeder memory.

PM: Mm-hm. What do you feel when you think of that memory?
CL: Kind of alone, isolated.

> This is yet another feeling that further confuses the issue. In addition to fear and feeling trapped, the feeling here is of feeling alone. Although these emotions are not unrelated, it seems significant that the one she chooses to indicate as most prominent changes from one event to the other.

PM: And what do you feel in your body, when you think of that memory?
CL: I keep having a spasm in my neck. Just that aloneness, just kind of all by myself.
PM: Mm-hm. So just sort of notice what you feel in your body now, as you sit here talking to me.
CL: Mm-hm.
PM: And then think of being four or five in the carport. And notice any change in your body.

> Sometimes clients propose negative or positive cognitions that they entertain in a global sense (like a schema), but that are not really directly connected specifically to the target memory. This is a good way to check: ask the client to think of the statement and ask herself how true it feels; then ask her to continue to think of it, and also think of the target memory, and see if the felt sense of its

Floatback To Four Years Old 105

truth changes when she goes from not thinking of the target event to thinking of it.

CL: It's more down here.
PM: It's more in your gut. So it's really in a different place, huh? But it's a strong feeling.
CL: Yeah, and I still have this neck thing too.
PM: Hm. So what I'm thinking right now is, for whatever reason, that's a powerful memory and worth processing. And I'm not sure if it's related to what we started with. It may or not be, but it seems like it's different physical sensations, somewhat different emotion.

> After a floatback, the memory that was identified must be checked to see if it really is a feeder for the later memory. To be a feeder, the earlier memory must have a similar body sensation associated with it, and similar emotion. In addition, it should be at least as disturbing as the later one (See Chapter One for exceptions), and must entail the same kind of disturbance. It seems pretty clear that this memory in the carport fails many of these tests. On the other hand, even if it is not a feeder for the incident with her husband, it may be a useful target in its own right, even if for a later processing session.

CL: Yeah.
PM: 0-10, how strong is that early one?
CL: Four.
PM: Four, wow. Looks like more than a four.

> I tend to reflect back what I see, especially if it is discordant with what the client is reporting. The client may not accept my impressions as accurate, in which case I am certainly not going to argue about it, but my feedback often helps a client to become aware of affect she was not aware of.

CL: Does it?
PM: Yeah. And how strong is the first marriage one?

CL: Six.

> Because the 4 or 5 year old memory does not seem to be a feeder to the recent one, it doesn't serve as the target we need, so we will go back to the memory from her first marriage, which has the same feeling, according to the client, and may be a feeder. I am not comfortable, however, until I understand enough about the targets that I can see why one would be a feeder for the other. My thought is that if a floatback from the first marriage memory will produce an earlier memory that makes sense as a feeder, I do not need to take more time trying to understand how the memory from her first marriage fits with the original incident.

PM: Uh-huh. And let's go back to that first marriage one. You're sitting on the porch. You remember looking down and having this feeling, "What have I done." And do you still have those physical sensations in your chest and your throat?
CL: It's up here now, yeah.
PM: Uh-huh. Ok. So just notice those sensations, and let your mind float back to an earlier memory. What's the first one that came up?
CL: It's not really going anywhere.
PM: Not going anywhere.
CL: Mm-hm.
PM: And the emotion is still there. And when you connect to the emotion, what age do you associate with that emotion?

> The "somatic bridge" form of floatback in which the client is asked to connect to the body sensation associated with the recent event and then let her mind float back to an early memory is especially powerful because it bypasses the left brain, so it is likely to pick up implicit memories that a left brain scan would miss. When the somatic bridge is not yielding a memory, an alternate strategy, which is still a right brain scan because it is not keyed to anything verbal, is to ask "What age does that feeling feel like?" and then "Can you think of being that age?" (See Chapter One for subtleties.)

Floatback To Four Years Old 107

CL: For some reason I want to say 13.
PM: Uh-huh. Ok. And when you think of a 13 year-old, what do you think of?
CL: Awkwardness.
PM: Uh-huh.
CL: Not really belonging. Wanting to belong.
PM: Uh-huh. So that sounds like that is sort of connected to the experience with your first husband?

> This is a question, because I really don't see it clearly myself.

CL: Maybe. Maybe, "How I got myself into this situation," yeah.
PM: So that marriage didn't exactly happen as a free choice?
CL: Yeah, I think I was trying to escape, and got myself somewhere worse. One of those.
PM: Uh-huh. Ok. So, "got myself somewhere worse," means someplace where you didn't feel you belong? Or you felt scared?
CL: Yeah, there's the fear thing there. Not measuring up. Not being good enough.

> To me fear, and not measuring up and not being good enough are quite different. The client is saying this as if it all seems to come together as one theme for her. At this point she has mentioned fear, feeling trapped, feeling alone, not measuring up and not being good enough. These fit together in some very loose way, but I look for targets that make good sense when processing begins, so that they will process in a way that makes sense and leads to resolution. The best organization I can bring to this sequence is that she started by identifying fear, and then all of her comments have been in the area of responsibility. I imagine that she has a distorted sense of responsibility, and she sees responsibility as being dangerous. This needed to be sorted out.

PM: Mm-hm. So the general theme with the first memory, it seems to be in the area of responsibility.
CL: Yeah, I was going to say, "Displeasing people."
PM: Uh-huh. And you said you were escaping from the situation, so is that the theme from this situation you were escaping from?
CL: Yeah. My sense I'm getting is, "being controlled." And wanting to escape that.
PM: Being controlled. I'm still thinking back to your experience with your current relationship, and there's a sense of, "Uh oh. I did something."
CL: I've done something I shouldn't have done. Yeah that being controlled has so many rules and requirements. And having to kind of walk the line and try not to upset anything, so maybe that fits.
PM: Yeah, so it sounds like that was a theme in your life.
CL: Mm-hm. Yeah.
PM: So when you think of an early representative experience of that theme, what do you think of?
CL: Sitting on the bleachers during physical education because I wasn't allowed to dance, and they were dancing in PE. That's what came to me.

> Having exhausted right brained scans, the next step is to float back on a negative cognition or in this case a "theme." (Floating back on a negative cognition is what is recommended in Shapiro's book (1995, 2001)

PM: Ah ha. And did that give you a sense of a lack of freedom?
CL: Yeah.
PM: And doing something wrong?
CL: Not in that case. That one connects more with the carport, being alone and different.

> Alone and different does not seem to relate to the recent experience with her husband, but she seems to be saying it does

relate to "doing something wrong." I am finding her statements to still be confusing.

PM: Different. Yeah.
CL: Alone. Outside.
PM: Yeah. If you would tie them all together, they would have to do with a lack of entitlement.

> This is a stretch, but the various memories that have come up seem diffuse and relatively unrelated. In hindsight, I regret bringing in "entitlement" as one more dimension to an already confusing discussion. I'm now thinking that the memories she has provided are really for the most part unrelated, or at least not part of the same cluster of events (not feeders for each other), and I should not be trying to work them into a single cluster. The client's response to her husband's annoyance seems quite irrational, and one would expect that it is not the first time she started to expect blame when someone had been angry and she had had nothing to do with the problem. The question we want to answer is, "where and when did this pattern begin?" That would be our ideal target.

CL: Mm-hm. Yeah. So, I don't deserve…
PM: Yeah, that's what it's sounding like. And right now your disturbance level is?
CL: After thinking about all of that right now? (Laughs) I think I'm up to a seven.
PM: Yeah, that's what I would've thought. So if we were to process that feeling of lacking entitlement, the problem might be that it's lifelong.
CL: Mm-hm.
PM: And it even precedes the memory from age four or five.
CL: Not really low-hanging fruit. (Laughs)

> The concept of "low-hanging fruit" in target selection is described in Chapter One.

PM: Well, not really low-hanging fruit. But that doesn't mean that it's not workable.
CL: Okay.

> Given all the different seemingly poorly related memories, I chose to punt, picking the four or five year old memory, because it was the earliest and the one closest to the theme of feeling like she is doing something wrong and will get in trouble. It is unclear if this is a feeder memory for the original one with her husband; however, with a memory from four or five years old, the first order of business is to see whether there is a need for additional resourcing.

VERIFYING ADEQUACY OF RESOURCES:

PM: But then the issue, what I would want to check out is, if you would think of that four-year-old. Can you picture her?
CL: Mm-hm.
PM: Tell me what you see.
CL: She's kind of cute, really.
PM: Uh-huh.
CL: Just a cute little four year old kid out there in the carport.
PM: Uh-huh. And literally what do you see? What's she wearing? What's her hair like?
CL: A short shoulder length, with bangs pulled back in a barrette. Shorts. T-shirt.
PM: What color?

> She has given a rich set of visual details, indicating to me that she is really seeing the image. Although apparently unnecessary in this particular case, I often ask a question about a relatively unimportant visual detail, like the color of someone's shirt or the

color of the wall, to determine if the client is actually seeing the image.

CL: White.
PM: You see that?
CL: Yeah. I'm thinking it's not a really good choice for me. It won't stay white. (Laughs)
PM: Uh-huh. But you smiled when you saw that. So you get some good feeling when you picture her.

> Always acknowledge indications of positive affect when focusing on resources. Clients are often unaware of the pleasurable feelings they experience when bringing a resource to mind. Acknowledging them seems to strengthen the connection the client feels between the resource and the associated positive affect.

CL: Mm-hm.
PM: And could you imagine holding her and comforting her?
CL: Mm-hm.
PM; So, that's easy to do. So, that's a good indication, that it's likely to process. I guess, what would make…I'm talking half to the class and half to you right now. What would make that a better target would be a specific moment in time. Why that moment of looking in the cage?
CL: We had a lot of animals. We were living in Texas, near my grandparents. They lived out in the country and we'd go see them on weekends. My dad would go walking in the woods at night, and he'd bring back baby animals. We had squirrels and raccoons. So the squirrels kind of fit with that period in my life. I can't really see the squirrels though; I just see the cage and the carport.
PM: So no sense about what…
CL: Yeah, I just got a flash of wanting to go inside, and my mom told me I had to stay outside. I couldn't come in.
PM: Ah.

CL: So maybe that's why that connected.
PM: So your mom had told you, you had to go outside, and you couldn't come in.
CL: Kind of a "get out of my hair thing," I think.
PM. Uh-huh. And that wasn't the first time?

> I ask this question to find out if there is probably an earlier memory feeding this one. If the child was surprised by the way her mother acted, there was probably not an earlier similar occurrence.

CL: It doesn't sound really typical of my mom.
PM: Oh, is that right?
CL: She might have just been overwhelmed at that point.

> Since this is an unusual behavior for mom, I am assuming that this memory does not connect back to earlier ones, and can be processed.

PM: Oh okay. Not typical. So her doing that, which is not a typical thing, brought up this feeling of not belonging.
CL: Yeah.
PM: Uh-huh. And I guess your mom was being a little cross with you. And your husband was angry.
CL: Yeah, and I didn't know why. And it was my fault. Yeah, okay.
PM: Uh-huh. Ok. So that's making sense. And when you think of that memory now, and you think of your mother being cross with you, what do you feel in your body?
CL: Yeah, now it's more of that same. Up higher.

> So, this early memory is beginning to sound more like a feeder for the recent one. Similar negative cognition, similar physical sensation, and both involving the same response to someone's anger.

Floatback To Four Years Old

PM: Good. So that sounds like that would be a good target.
CL: Okay.
PM: It sounds like, if not low-hanging fruit, it's not too high up in the tree either.
CL: Okay.
PM: Especially since you're resourced. You have a positive feeling about...Is it a four year old, or a five year old?
CL: Probably four.
PM: Four years old. Ok. Well, usually there's a clock on the wall (referring to the classroom). We could process it if you want. Would you like to?
CL: If you think it would be good, yeah.
PM: I think it would work, and be useful.
CL: Ok.
PM: But I don't have a wand, and I'm afraid to get up (difficult to get up because of all the microphone wires). (Client laughs) Ok. So you have this feeling already in your chest and throat. Do you have an image that relates to your mom being cross?
CL: Just that moment. I'm standing in the door, with the door open, starting to go in and she's stopping me.
PM: Oh, ok.

> This is a new image, and one that would be expected to be connected to the feelings involved. So, it is a better image to begin targeting with.

CL: I can't really see her face.
PM: Yeah, and you have the sensation of actually holding the door.

> EMDR is most effective when the client can connect strongly to the target in an affective way. Any additional senses that can be brought into the targeting, like smell, taste or physical sensation will make the target more accessible. If available to the client, they should be brought into stronger focus by a comment from the

therapist. In this case, a gesture on the part of the client indicated that she was recalling the experience of holding the door.

CL: Mm-hm.
PM: Good, and the negative thought about yourself is, "I must have done something wrong"?
CL: Yeah. It must be my fault.
PM: "It must be my fault." And the positive is what?
CL: It's not my fault. She's just...
PM: It's not about me.
CL: Yeah.
PM: So the positive would be, "I'm okay."

> This point is very minor. Shapiro lists "It's not my fault" in her text (1995, 2001) as an acceptable positive cognition. I prefer "I'm okay" if it applies, because it is more grounded in the present, whereas "It's not my fault" is often taken to mean, "It wasn't my fault," which is focused on the past. People who think "It's my fault" usually think "It's my fault and so I'm not okay."

CL: Mm-hm.
PM: And how true does that feel, on a gut level, when you think of the memory? How true does it feel now? "I'm okay."
CL: I forgot what's...
PM: I haven't given you the scale.

> I often simplify the VOC question by initially omitting the 1 to 7 scale. Then, when the client tells me how true it feels, I ask what that would be "on a scale of 1 to 7 where 7 is completely true and 1 is completely untrue."

CL: It's true. It's not really connected with my...How true does it feel?
PM: When you think of the memory.
CL: Mm-hm. It's kind of in the middle.

Floatback To Four Years Old 115

PM: In the middle. So on s scale of 1-7, 7 is completely true and 1 is completely false, that would be?
CL: About a 4.
PM: A four. Ok. The emotions coming up now, when you think of the memory? What emotions are coming up?
CL: It's hard to put a name to it. The closest I can get is fear.
PM: Fear. Ok. No sadness?
CL: Some sadness, but more fear.
PM: More fear. Ok.
CL: Not knowing.
PM: Okay. Good. Guilt? Shame?

> If there are feelings that I would expect to be part of a target, I usually ask the client if they apply. If the client answers affirmatively, usually the target becomes more lit up. I would expect a target where a major issue is fault to involve guilt or shame. If the client indicated this not to be the case, I would wonder if the negative cognition was an accurate one.

CL: Mm-hm. Guilt.
PM: Guilt. Ok. You can feel that now?
CL: Mm-hm.
PM: And you're feeling all of that in your body, in your chest?
CL: Here.
PM: And your throat also, or mostly in your chest now?
CL: Mostly chest now.

DESENSITIZATION AND REPROCESSING:

PM: Ok, so I just want you to just notice that sensation, and that memory of standing at the door, holding the door, and your mother telling you to "stay out. You can't come in." And the thought, "I must've done something. It's my fault." Have you got all that?

I always pause before starting the initial set of bilateral stimulation to see if the client is sufficiently connected to the target. Putting together these three diverse aspects of the target representing different sensory modes takes a bit of time and effort and it is necessary to wait until they are all actively accessed (equivalent to "ringing the bell" – referred to in Chapter One)

CL: Yeah.

PM: Ok. So just notice <><> Just notice what's coming up. Just notice. That's right. That's good. Just notice. Just notice. That's right. Good. Good. Good. Just notice. That's right. That's right. That's good. Just notice. Good. Good. Good. That's right. Good. So blank it out now, and take a deep breath. What's coming up now?

CL: It's just…It's not fair. And I'm out here all by myself, and it's not fair.

PM: Mm-hm. Think of that. <><> Just notice. That's right. That's good. Just notice. Just notice. That's right. That's good. That's right. Right. Good. That's good. That's right. Good. Good. Good. Blank it out now, and take a deep breath. What's coming up now?

CL: I've kind of found myself back in front of the squirrel cage, and I was trying to figure out why I couldn't see the squirrels. I know there are squirrels in there.

> The client has slipped into present tense ("I'm out here all by myself," "I'm back in front of the squirrel cage," "I know there are squirrels in there.") indicating she is losing adult perspective.

PM: Hm. Ok. Just notice that. <><> Blank it out, take a deep breath.

CL: The feeling of being stuck. Like I'm stuck out here, I can't go inside. I don't have anything to do; I'm just stuck out here on the outside.

> The client is now talking entirely in present tense. Talking in present tense may indicate that the client is not aware of her present adult perspective when thinking of the child experience.

Floatback To Four Years Old 117

> This can interfere with integrating child perspective with an adaptive adult perspective and cause processing to stall, or in the case of highly dissociative clients even allow the client to slip into an overwhelmed child-like state. I decided to play it safe by directing the client back to target.

PM: So go back to the memory now. And how disturbing is it now, on a scale of 0-10?
CL: A three.
PM: You said it was a 7 when you started?
CL: Yeah, cause we had everything all at once (laughs).

> This appears to mean that the client is not holding all the aspects of the target at once now.

PM: It was going up and down, yeah. So what do you think it was when we started?
CL: I think it was probably a 5 or 6 at the start of it.
PM: Ok. And what was responsible for the change? Why is it less disturbing now?

> I like this question, when I have not heard the adult perspective that helped the client feel less disturbed. Often it simply was not verbalized, but, when I ask, the client can tell me right away. Sometimes, the client cannot tell me and then I explore further to try to understand what is responsible for the lower report of SUDS. (See Chapter One for a more complete discussion.)

CL: All I can come up with is that I've moved away from the door, and back just out to look at the squirrels. So, acceptance. This is how it is, kind of.
PM: I'm trying to track when you're being that four year old, and when you're here thinking of the four year old. So, as you sit here and think of the four-year old, what stands out for you now?

> This is an attempt to make sure the reduction in disturbance is not caused by some form of dissociation, which would be suggested by the previous examples of the client slipping into present tense.

CL: She didn't do anything. She didn't do anything wrong.

> This appears to be a solid adaptive adult perspective. She is now seeing the situation through the eyes of a reasonable and compassionate adult.

PM: Just think of that. <><> Blank it out and take a deep breath. And what are you noticing now?
CL: Just the thought that it's not my problem. It was her problem.

> This seems to represent solid adaptive adult perspective. The generic resolution for a distortion in the area of responsibility is the realization "This is not about me."

PM: Think of that. <><> Blank it out and take a deep breath.
CL: I started to feel angry.
PM: Uh-huh.
CL: This wasn't my fault and yet I was stuck out there, and couldn't go inside.

> When clients start out feeling angry in addressing a target memory, I am usually suspect. Anger is usually not a primary emotion related to a target, but is a more comfortable emotion to feel than, for example, helplessness, so the client's initial focus on anger is usually a defense against more uncomfortable feelings. When processing has moved along, however, and the disturbance level has dropped, as it has here, I find that anger may come up and represent an adult perspective. In my experience, this normally indicates that processing is well along its way to resolution.

PM: Think of that. <><> Blank it out and take a deep breath.

CL: I thought how life's just not fair. And then I was thinking about how much my kids hated that when I used to tell them that (laughs).
PM: (laughs) Think of that. <><> Blank it out, and take a deep breath.
CL: I was trying to think what I would tell my four-year-old self about it. It wasn't her fault. But she's still stuck out there. And to just watch the squirrels and enjoy myself until I could go back in, I guess. It's not my fault.
PM: It's not about her.

> This is the generic concept for inappropriate attribution of responsibility! Her comment is reminiscent of a distortion that is common with clients and that also sometimes confuses therapists as well: "But she's still stuck out there." In this case the client is considering how to help the four-year-old come to terms with this unfair situation. In general, we need to remember that we are not trying to correct what happened back then; all we can do is correct the way the client presently holds what happened in her mind. In this case, she is addressing the child's feeling that she has done something wrong, not trying to vainly find a way to get the child back into the house.

CL: Yeah.
PM: <><> What's coming up now?
CL: Not really much. Just the same. It's not my fault.

> Even though the client seemed to be saying the right things, I did not see a full resolution happening. The child she was describing did not seem entirely onboard with the new adaptive adult perspective. The client seems to be going back and forth between viewing the child through the eyes of an adult and identifying with her child self. ("It's not my fault.") I decided it would be helpful to utilize the adult client directly as a resource, making the child less isolated and keeping the client clear about when she is in her adult perspective and when she is identifying with the child.

UTILIZATION OF RESOURCE

PM: Mm-hm. What do you think that four year old needs from you?
CL: Not to feel so alone.
PM: Right. So what would she need?
CL: Companionship. I don't know.
PM: Uh-huh. So what would she need from you, as an adult, to do if you were there?
CL: Give her a hug.
PM: Mm-hm. Think of that. <><> What are you noticing now?

> I did not find many significant changes between Shapiro's first edition (1995) and her second edition (2001), but this seems to be a significant one. In the section on cognitive interweave, she offers the possibility that the client might insert her adult self into the initial disturbing target scene and help the child to address the situation. She also suggests that if the client does not spontaneously imagine physically comforting the child, the therapist might suggest that the client might want to imagine herself as an adult putting her arm around the child. This seems to be very effective in memories in which the cognitive distortion is primarily in the area of responsibility.

CL: It felt like that's what I needed.

> The client is speaking in first person ("I"). She seems to be pretty well grounded in her adult self, but it nevertheless, makes sense to respond to her by referring to the child in third person. This will help her to keep from slipping into identifying overly with the child, and losing her present grounding in her adult self.

PM: Yeah. Maybe she needs to hear what a sweet kid she is. How loveable she is. How cute she is. You think so?
CL: Yeah.
PM: <><> What's coming up now?

Floatback To Four Years Old

CL: I started to feel sadness. That I just didn't have someone to give me that at that point.

> At this point I might have asked, "Who is feeling that sadness, the child or you, the adult?" This question tends to connect the client to her adult compassionate self, as opposed to her identification with the neglected or helpless child.

PM: Mm-hm. Just notice that <><>. What's coming up now?
CL: I was thinking about all the things my parents did do that showed me that I was loved, and that they cared. And that was just really one isolated unusual incident.
PM: Think of that. <><> And what are you noticing now?
CL: I remember this skunk. It was the same age. I had the mumps, I think, and I was waiting for my dad to come home from work, because I just wanted him to hold me because I was so miserable, and he had been sprayed by a skunk, so being in his lap was not nearly as comforting as I thought. (Laughs)

> In this case the client is moving away from the original target, probably because it is no longer significantly disturbing.

PM: (laughs) Just think of all that. <><> What's coming up now?
CL: It feels good to laugh about it. It's funny looking back.
PM: Think about that. <><> What are you noticing now?
CL: I was just thinking, "Really, overall, I did have a happy childhood."

> One of the beauties of processing trauma is that, as they stop avoiding the trauma memory, clients can also begin to access positive memories that may surround the trauma memory. What wonders can be done for a client's depression when she starts to remember positive events and recognizes that she was in fact a happy child.

PM: Mm-hm. Just think of that. <><> What are you noticing now?
CL: Just feeling better. Being able to see the whole picture instead of just that one.
PM: Larger perspective. Yeah. So go back to the memory now. How disturbing is it, on a scale of 0-10?
CL: Maybe a one.
PM: Maybe a one. And what makes it maybe a one?
CL: There's still that frustration of I really wanted to go inside, and I can't. It's more like, okay. It's not about me anymore.

> The client is confusing then with now. "I really wanted to go inside" refers to the frustration she felt as a child. Is it still disturbing for her now as an adult when she thinks about that memory? Probably not. The fact that she was frustrated at the time will not change, just as the fact that she was unable to go inside will never change. If this is producing a disturbance at a level of 1 NOW, there must be something about the child not being able to go inside that is disturbing NOW. For instance, perhaps the client still has this sense that she can never get what she wants. If so, that would be another negative cognition (cognitive distortion). It is possible that the frustration is only in the past, and that in present time the memory had ceased to be disturbing at all.

PM: Think of that. <><> Blank it out, and take a deep breath.
CL: I just had this thought of sometimes, you just need to take a deep breath and watch the squirrels for a while.
PM: So how disturbing is the memory now?
CL: It doesn't feel like it is anymore.

INSTALLATION:

PM: Hm. So what about the statement, "I'm okay." How true does that feel, on a gut level, when you think of the memory?
CL: It feels true.

Floatback To Four Years Old

PM: On a scale of 1-7, it's a 6 or 7?

CL: Seven, yeah.

PM: Seven. Ok, so think of the memory, and that statement, "I'm ok." Tell me when you've got them both.

CL: Okay.

PM: Ok. <><> Blank it out, and take a deep breath. What's coming up now?

CL: A sense of peacefulness. It's just okay.

BODY SCAN:

PM: And if you close your eyes and scan your body. Notice any unpleasant sensation?

CL: Still just a little bit here.

PM: Your stomach. And what about your chest and throat? (Client shakes her head "no"). No, it's your stomach. Well, just notice that sensation in your stomach. <><> Blank it out, and take a deep breath. What are you noticing now?

CL: It's just about gone.

PM: It's just about gone. It changed?

CL: Yeah.

PM: Ok, so notice the change. <><> And what are you noticing?

CL: Feeling real hypnotic. Kind of trance-like.

> Based on the process that I was seeing, and my sense of the client being very grounded, I was not worried that her hypnotic trance-like feeling was an indication of dissociation.

PM: Uh-huh. Nothing else. What about your stomach?

> Often, when I want to make sure a client's issue is resolved, I will attempt to verify that all aspects of the target are indeed resolved by asking specifically about various things that the client has mentioned as emotional triggers related to disturbance.

CL: It's not there. It's gone.

PM: Not there. Good. So I think that's a good place for us to stop. I think that there may be some pieces to work on in the practicum. I think we worked on a very select slice of it. It seems like there was another theme that was in it when we were talking about it. And so that may be something that you want to process in the practicum.

CL: Ok.

PM: But let me check, when you think about your husband looking for his keys. How disturbing is that now?

> When a target being processed was originally identified as a feeder for a recent incident, I always check the disturbance on the recent incident to see if it too has lost it's disturbing charge.

CL: Not nearly as much. Maybe like a 2.

PM: A two. Ok. So that's interesting. So you could just process that directly in the practicum, but then you have this other piece that kind of goes back to your childhood that you would process also. But I would feel good about the processing we did. I feel like we took a nice select confined piece, and we processed it. Well, good. Thank you for being willing to do this.

> This is an example of how the three pronged protocol works. First we took the most recent memory, found the earliest related experience, and processed it. In the next session we would process the most recent memory if it was still disturbing, and finally we would process a future template. The future template, in this case, would probably be to image a future situation in which her husband becomes angry about something having nothing to do with her. As far as I know, she did not continue to process this material during the practicum, and she indicated at 2.5 year follow-up that the original issue was completely resolved.

CL: Thank you.

End of session.

TWO YEAR FOLLOWUP:

All I can remember of it now is just a visual image of standing in the carport outside our kitchen door. There's not much detail to the image, nothing happening, except there's sunshine, and the carport, and the door, and me. Emotionally, it's pretty neutral. It's just sort of a snapshot image of a moment in time, with nothing really attached to it. It's interesting, now that you ask (about the effect on the presenting problem). I can't remember the last time I had that "it's my fault" inner cringing reaction to being around someone who is angry. And that used to be a pretty significant thing for me. How about that! :)

6

Inadequate Preparation

(Video #10 in JFKU site)

This was an attempt to process a memory that had been unsuccessfully processed in a practicum session the previous day. The client's presenting issue had floated back to a memory of listening, as a very young child (2 or 3 years old), to Mom and Dad fighting and hearing crashing and being terrified. As is the case with most memories from that age, there were previous incidents, which were probably feeder memories for the one that was being processed, although the client was unable to specifically identify them. Occurring earlier than 3 years old, they were no-doubt pre-verbal memories which would be difficult to work with, and would very likely require multiple sessions to process. Given the limited nature of an in-class demonstration session, the limited time for processing, the lack of adequate follow-up, the lack of a thorough history, and the lack of time for resourcing, I would have been prudent to forego processing of this memory. I did, however, attempt some trauma processing. Although the client's follow-up assessment of the session was that it was helpful, the session is a good example of the difficulties a memory of this type presents without adequate history taking, resourcing and other preparation. (59 minutes)

CL: Coming to the seminar this week, there's been a lot of stressful events that have happened; all of the same theme. So yesterday I was able to identify that there was a memory of something that happened to me as a teenager, and then we did a float back to an earlier memory where I was two or three years old.

PM: Ok, so two or three years old. I can understand why that didn't process very well in practicum. So what did you decide to do about this two or three year old memory?

CL: To do the container exercise. Want me to talk about that?

> The client is referring to an exercise that is commonly used to close down an incomplete session by imagining all the disturbing material and associations being put into a secure container, to be taken out a bit at a time for processing in future sessions.

PM: Ok, so you did the container, and so the reason we're doing this today is that you're thinking, "I had this target that didn't get processed. Is that right?

CL: Yes.

PM: Ok, so. I'm not likely to want to target something from two or three years old here, for the same reason that you wouldn't want to do it in a practicum. But if you can explain to me what the targets were, then I can sort of decide for myself.

CL: The actual target memory or the cognition?

PM: No, the target memory.

CL: The target memory. As a teenager?

PM: Start with that.

CL: I was standing at the kitchen sink doing dishes, I was sixteen or seventeen years old, and I let out a big sigh. (Client sighs.) And my mom came in from the other room as I was doing that, and she looked at me and said, "What is your problem? You act like you have the weight of the world on your shoulders." And I just didn't turn to look at her. I just kept doing the dishes.

PM: So you just got teary, and on the face of it, this memory doesn't sound like something that would bring up as strong of a response as you have, so I'd like to understand more about your response.

Inadequate Preparation

CL: I think the deep sigh represented a lot of stress that I was feeling from what was going on in the household at the time. Dad's an alcoholic, a lot of, just, stress.
PM: Right, but the emotion that just came up about your mother saying "What's wrong with you? You act like you have the weight of the world on your shoulders."
CL: Like it wasn't okay to have feelings. It wasn't okay to be distressed about anything.
PM: So what you're saying is this is how you interpreted your mother's comment? (Client nods) So your mother says, "What's wrong with you?" And then you say to yourself "She's telling me it's not okay to have feelings."

> This statement has the appearance of a straight-forward negative cognition.

CL (Nods)
PM: And the emotion that just came up with you now was having to deal with feeling like you were getting this message that it wasn't okay to have feelings. Is that right?
CL: I guess so. Like I didn't matter. Like it was better if I just didn't comment on anything, or, yeah, have feelings.

> In hindsight, I should have known even this early in the process that this memory was probably not an appropriate target until more careful history taking and case conceptualization was done. Feelings of "I don't matter" and "It's not okay to have feelings" would not have begun during teen years. These messages usually start very young, often preverbal.

PM: Why is that so emotional now when you think about it?
CL: I don't know. Other than just the previous memories that I floated back to.
PM: So when you floated back, did you float back on a physical sensation?

CL: I think so. This week we talked about how I was feeling tightness in my stomach and in my throat, and I wanted to just cry. Just get the bubbles of the soap, and just wanted to sob. And then just on that, I went back to that two or three year old.

> Therapists should be cautious about floating back on a physical sensation where there is no context or content related to it. Floatbacks of this sort can lead anywhere, including memories that may overwhelm the client or memories that are too general or broad in nature to make good targets.

PM: So the wanting to sob; what was that feeling?
CL: Right now, I'm just feeling really angry at my mom.

> Here, there is again a sense that the client's feelings are general and only loosely related to the memory being discussed. The present tense delivery also suggests that the client is not currently grounded in her present adult self.

PM: Yeah.
CL: And I'm just feeling that my parents were never there for me emotionally, ever.

> Global statements like this are not tied to a particular event, although it is sometimes possible to find a source event. In this case the client has already placed the source material as being preverbal. Again, preverbal material can be worked with, but not without history taking and preparation in the form of self-regulation skills and resourcing, and, needless to say, not in a one hour demonstration session in front of a class.

PM: So when your mother says, "What's wrong with you? You look like you have the weight of the world on your shoulders."
CL: Sound like...

Inadequate Preparation 131

PM: Sound like. Because of the sigh. Then your thought is thinking about that your parents were never there for you. Is that right?
CL: Yeah. Like I didn't matter. Like I was a bother to them. Like I was in the way. They had too many other things going on, and it was just more stressful to have kids, even though they wanted twelve of them. (Laughs)
PM: Did you have…
CL: They had four in five years. They stopped after four. So we were close together. It was a lot.
PM: And how old were you when you were doing the dishes? You told me, but I forgot.
CL: Sixteen, I think.
PM: Ok, so I'll tell you my thought process here. And I'm thinking sixteen, fifteen, fourteen; those are ages when it's pretty common that adolescents become angry. So something that was just hurtful before or something that would make you feel bad about yourself, and you get to a certain age and it's not just that you feel bad. Now you feel angry because you're more aware that something is being done to you. Is that right?

> This might be a plausible explanation of why a teenage memory that has a similar theme to very early memories might still be possible to process without first addressing the early memories. It does happen that later memories can sometimes have an additional dimension to them that comes from unique aspects of the later event or the more advanced age of the client at that time. In other words, there may be additional channels or a somewhat unique perspective to the later memory that enables it to be processed either wholly or in part without first processing the earlier memories. For instance, a client has a long history of being terrified by her father's explosive anger and by loud fights between mom and dad, but then there is a later incident in which dad has pulled a knife and is holding it to mom's throat and threatening to kill her. This later incident certainly has a similar theme to incidents of loud fighting, but it also has a new element

that involves the knife and threat of death, making it a somewhat distinct target. My rule of thumb is that, if the more recent event is sufficiently disturbing in its own right, and does not need the earlier memories to generate the level of disturbance that it does, it can probably be processed separately. Similarly, if the SUDS on the later incident is greater than the earlier ones, it may be possible to process it separately. In retrospect, however, the above explanation does not seem sound when applied to this client, since the client's global descriptions of the disturbance suggest that this later memory is just part of a cluster of memories that began much earlier.

CL: Yes. There's probably an element of that. Huh! Yeah. (Laughs)
PM: So you had the tension in your belly, and you floated back on that. And what came up?

FOCUSING THE TARGET:

CL: I'm sitting at the top of the stairs with two of my other siblings, we're a year apart; eighteen months apart. We're all in our jammies, it's at night, and Mom and Dad are downstairs yelling and fighting and the door is closed at the bottom of the stairs.

> Note that the client is again speaking in present tense, as if she is having the experience now. The problem with this is potentially that she loses awareness of her present adult perspective.

PM: So primarily this memory is hearing sounds of fighting, and being very small, and you're saying you're earlier than three. It's more like two years old?
CL: I think I'm three, because my sister is on this side, and she had to have been two because she's old enough to sit. And my other brother is four on this side.
PM: So when you think of that memory, you get the same physical sensation in your belly?

Inadequate Preparation

CL: I did yesterday, and I think we processed it through to a certain degree. And then when I just let myself really get into that scene, like later when we were talking about it, it seemed to trigger back up when I remembered about hearing the sound of a plate crashing on the other side of the door. So things were being thrown then, and that retriggered again that...

PM: So that brings up feeling now. Is that right?

CL: Yeah.

PM: And what does it mean to you, the sound of plates crashing?

CL: Someone is getting hurt on the other side, and nobody is stopping it.

PM: So in your three-year-old mind, I assume you assume mother is getting hurt. Is that right?

CL: I think so, yeah.

PM: Okay, and how disturbing is that feeling now, on a scale of 0-10?

CL: I want to say seven.

PM: Seven. How disturbing is the original memory? You said it was more than seven, right?

CL: Yeah, like an eight or nine.

WRONG FLOATBACK MEMORY:

PM: So, it sounds like they're not exactly related, the two memories. The first memory you're feeling like you're kind of a burden, and you're not allowed to have feeling, and it reminds you of your parents not being there for you. And in your early memory, it's fear that someone is getting hurt. Is that right?

CL: I think so, yes.

PM: *The one is probably not exactly a feeder for the other.* The more recent memory, it's certainly not low-hanging fruit because what you're saying is that it's representative of a lifelong experience of your feelings not being welcome, and you feeling neglected by your parents. Is that right?

> The concept of "low-hanging fruit" in EMDR target selection is discussed in Chapter One.

CL: (nods) yes.
PM: So ironically, in my mind, the memory of standing at the sink would be harder to process than the memory of sitting on the stairs during the mayhem. Does that make sense?

> This comment was off. The early memory, as noted several times in these pages, is not likely to be easily processed without additional preparation.

CL: Yes.
PM: So if we were to process standing at the sink, then basically what's going to come up is lots of experiences of being neglected. Now, often when children are hearing parents "going at it," they have this thought of, "I'm not important, I don't count." Is that part of that experience?

> This is a case where neither target should be processed in a demonstration situation. Even at three years old, the client has been frightened before by the parents' fighting. Memories involving earlier than three years old are very likely to be preverbal, and are, at the very least, going to require establishing a strong resource (adaptive adult perspective) before moving on to trauma processing.

CL: That's what we kind of determined yesterday when we went back to check the VOC, that I wasn't in agreement with the cognition yet. And that's where we felt that we hadn't completely processed everything yet.
PM: So the positive cognition was "My feelings matter." And it didn't feel entirely true when you thought of the memory.
CL: Yeah.
PM: And the unfinished part of the process seemed to be the sound.

Inadequate Preparation   135

CL: I think the words we used for the cognition were, "I'm insignificant," versus, "I have significance," or, "I am significant."
PM: Ok.
CL: The sound, yeah.
PM: And the fighting between your parents, was that unusual in some respect?
CL: I don't think it was unusual, but I think the intensity was that night. And I think that was the first time the three of us were gathered together. And we were talking about what we should do. And I felt like my older brother should go down and stop it. He was only four. I knew that was wrong at the time. And I think all three of us inched slowly down the stairs, and we'd run back up and climb back down them again. It was just this long process of back and forth.
PM: So even if your parents fought before that, there was something unique about this in that there was the sense that someone was getting hurt.
CL: Yes.
PM: And it would make sense that the children should do something.
CL: Yes.
PM: Ok. You said that was a seven. Now typically in a situation where you're hearing sounds and it scares you, typically you're sitting there having an image in your mind of what's going on out there. I'm wondering if you have an image. (Client nods) So what's the image?
CL: My dad being intoxicated, and my mom being angry, and (fighting back tears) them being physical with each other. I'm just assuming that they're hurting each other, and I'm seeing it. I can see that.

> "Dad being intoxicated and my mom being angry" is too general to be an actual image. If it were an actual image the client would be seeing someone getting hurt, and not need to "assume" it.

PM: So, I was going to say, you seem to be losing the image. What do you actually see now in the image?
CL: Just their faces.

PM: So the actual - someone getting hurt - the actual violence is not part of the image?
CL: I don't think so.
PM: You see both of their faces in one image?
CL: Yes.
PM: So how do you see that? If I had a photo, what would I be seeing?
CL: I'm on the other side of the door. Like I've opened the door, and I can see them yelling and screaming at each other, like a foot apart.
PM: So they're kind of in each other's faces.
CL: Right.
PM: But there are no dishes breaking.
CL: In that image; but I know it happened.

> Again, we want to encourage the client to be in the present moment and report what she actually sees in the image, and what she actually hears. If she knows that something happened at another time, like dishes crashing, it is not part of the moment in time that we are targeting, and it muddies the target to try to include it. On the other hand, the client becomes most emotional when she mentions the sound of the dishes crashing. Perhaps that sound is more important than the image that does not go with it.

PM: So as I sit here with you, and I look at you; you seem to have a much stronger reaction to the sound of the dishes breaking than you have to the image of the two of them being in each other's faces screaming. So I'm asking that when you bring back the sound of the dishes breaking, what image comes up? What captures that disturbance?
CL: Dad is hurting Mom, and Mom is trying to push him away, or fight him away, and just throw something. But it crashes instead of hitting him.
PM: Ok, so that image involves that Dad has physical contact with Mom, and Mom is trying to hit him with something.
CL: Yes.

Inadequate Preparation   137

PM: So it looks to me that the image you've got may not be crystal clear. You can't see what she's got in her hand exactly, but there is this image of the situation of emotions. And how disturbing is it now on a scale of 0-10?
CL sighs
PM: Nine?
CL: Ok. (Laughs)
PM: So it's gotten stronger?
CL: Yeah.
PM: Ok.
CL: Can I just add; beyond that event, beyond that part, at some point, I think we went down to the bottom of the stair and opened the door. And my mom came over and yelled at us for being out of bed. And told us to immediately go back upstairs and get in bed. And they shut the door on us again, but then the fight stopped after that, so then we were just dismissed. I just wanted to share that, because I don't know if that's related again to the…

> In the EMDR process, we try to identify a moment in time that captures the most disturbing part of the memory. This secondary event of opening the door and Mom yelling at them does not appear to be part of the most disturbing moment.

PM: So why is it that you wanted to share that?
CL: Because I feel seeing them argue and fight is a different feeling, and maybe a different cognition than the, "I'm not significant" distortion.
PM: Well, from my point of view, and this is a good example, by the way, the reason I keep asking the SUDS…it hasn't come yet in the actual assessment, but I ask so that I know what we're talking about. And it's really clear to me that part of this memory that has a big punch is hearing the crashing. So that's what we're going to process.
CL: Ok.
PM: And when you have that image of them in combat-- she's trying to hit him with something and he's grabbing her. I think that's what

you're saying. But anyway, they're in close combat, and it's reached a physical level, and when you have that image, what is the negative thought that comes to mind about yourself now?

> I am missing the apparent fact that the crashing of the dishes and the image of the parents in combat are separate, and the client is not really able to bring them together. The crashing seems to be more evocative of the disturbance than the image. The client is jumping from one idea to another, and it is understandably difficult to find a single focus for the disturbance associated with this memory. This is probably a result of the client's desire to avoid the intensity of the memory.

CL: It's hard to bring it back from, "nobody's safe" to just me. I feel powerless, when I think about it.
PM: So you're recalling the memory, and you're feeling powerless. You're feeling the powerlessness that you felt at the time. And the thought about yourself now; is that "I'm powerless?" Or is that just a thought that relates to the experience?
CL: Well, this week has felt "I'm powerless" a lot. (Laughs) But, yeah.
PM: I'm not getting it.

> The client has now jumped into present time, talking about the recent week. It is useful in identifying an appropriate negative cognition to make sure that the one that appears to be appropriate to the early floatback memory also applies to the recent memory from which she floated back. Normally, however, it is not the client but the therapist who is thinking about this. In this presentation, I can't keep up with all the jumps, and am voicing my confusion.

CL: How I feel about myself now?
PM: So what I'm asking is if you think of the memory, obviously you felt powerless at the time. You also felt some responsibility to fix the situation. It sounds like you also felt protective of your sister. So, there

was a lot of distortion. So the question is, what aspects of that distortion now carry through to your present adult self? So as you sit here in the chair, and you think of that memory, what's the negative thought that comes to your mind about yourself now?

> When there is confusion about whether the client is talking about a distortion relating to a past memory or the present (which we are trying to bring into focus), it is a good idea to make the intent clear with a phrase like "as you sit here in the chair."

CL: Like all three of those things. "I don't matter. I'm insignificant, and I'm powerless."
PM: Those have a ring of truth for you now as you sit here in the chair?
CL: That "I'm insignificant", and "I'm powerless."
PM: They have a ring of truth now? Now, when you think of the memory, then they get stronger?

> This is also a good test of a negative cognition. When the client thinks of the statement and then, while holding the statement in mind, thinks of the memory, the statement should feel viscerally truer.

CL: Yes.

POSITIVE COGNITION:

PM: Good. So rather than, "I'm insignificant and I'm powerless," what would you prefer to think about yourself now, when you think of that memory?
CL: That I am significant, and that I am capable.
PM: "I can make a difference?"
CL: That I can make a difference.
PM: Does that feel true when you think of the memory?
CL: Okay, yes.

PM: It feels relevant. Does it feel true when you think of the memory? How true does it feel about you now?

> I have a sense here that the client may not really be reporting a statement which she viscerally connects to the memory, so I keep checking in different ways.

CL: About me now, how true does it feel?
PM: "I can make a difference" and "I'm significant."
CL: "I can make a difference," and "I'm significant." Two.

> I often ask the VOC question in two parts. First I ask how true the statement feels, and then I ask the client to give it a rating from 1 to 7. In this case the client is taking the training and already knows the scale.

PM: So the scale is from 1-7. And seven is completely true, and so it's a two. Ok. And what are the emotions that are coming up when you think of that memory?

EMOTIONS:

CL: I don't know what you're asking. I'm sorry.
PM: The emotions that you feel now when you think of the memory.
CL: Hurt. Fear. Pain.
PM: Ok.
CL: Abandonment. I don't know what to say. I'm in emotional pain. (Laughs)
PM: You feel alone?

> As a rule, if there is an emotion I see on the client's face or have heard the client express previously in relation to the target event or would make sense in the context of what happened, I will ask the client if that emotion should also be included.

Inadequate Preparation

CL: Yeah, I feel alone.

PM: Ok. So, still a nine? Or has it changed considering that?

CL: We can keep it at a nine. (Laughs)

PM: Ok. And you were feeling it in your gut before. Where are you feeling it now in your body?

CL: Probably everywhere. But gut and throat.

PM: Ok. By the way, I want to check. (Turning to the class) Can people hear? It's good? Ok. So your gut and your throat. And can you feel that now?

CL: I just blanked it out, and took a deep breath. (Laughs)

PM: That's fine. Can you feel it now?

CL: Yes.

PM: Good. Just notice the feeling in your gut and in your throat, and that sound of the crashing, and the image of your parents being physically engaged in this conflict, and the thought "I'm insignificant, I'm powerless." Tell me when you have all that. Do you have it?

CL: (nods) Yes.

PM: Just follow the ball. <><> Just follow. Can you move your eyes? So is the wand threatening for you?

CL: It just was a little too close.

PM: I can move further away.

CL: Ok. I'm okay with where I'm at now.

PM: Ok. It might be hard to reach you with the microphone further away.

CL: Ok, then. Shorten it up please.

PM: Ok. I'll do that. (Wand is shortened)

> Normally this adjustment would have been made during the preparation phase.

PM: So tell me if this is okay.

CL: Once or twice. (PM moves the wand back and forth) Okay. Okay.

PM: Ok. So, go back to that feeling, that physical sensation, which was in your gut and someplace else?

CL: Throat.

PM: Throat, good. Just feel those sensations, the thought "I'm insignificant and powerless," the sound of the crashing, and that image of the two of them physically engaged. Do you have all of that?
CL: (nods)
PM: Ok. Just follow the ball. <><> Keep your eyes moving. Just notice. Just notice. Just notice. That's right. That's good. That's good. Just notice. That's right. That's right. You're doing fine. That's good. Good. That's right. Just notice. Just notice. That's right. That's good. Good. That's right. That's right. Just notice. Just notice. That's right. That's right. That's good. Just notice. Just notice. That's right. That's right. That's good. Good. Good. Just notice. Good. Blank it out, and take a deep breath. Tell me what's coming up.

> See the initial discussion in Chapter One of this volume about "cadence comments."

CL: I just want my mommy. And I want her to be okay. (Fairly emotional)

> This would have been a good time to take her back to target and help her to become grounded again in her present adult self. Whether the loss of adult awareness is a dissociative process, is not within the realm of this text to discuss, however this phenomenon is very relevant to how processing proceeds. "I just want my mommy," for instance, is an indication that she is losing connection with her adult self. Also, use of present tense indicates a blurring of the client's awareness of present and past. According to the Adaptive Information Processing Model, on which EMDR is conceptually based, resolution occurs as new neural pathways are laid down between the neural network representing the target memory and adaptive adult perspectives held in the rest of the informational system. (Shapiro, 1995, 2001) The client must simultaneously attend to the target memory as well as adult awareness. If the client is not at least partially connected to her adult observing self, these connections will not be made.

Inadequate Preparation 143

PM: You're feeling scared. Just notice that. <><> Just notice. That's good. Just notice. That's good. That's good. Just notice. Just notice. That's right. That's good. That's good. Good. That's right. Good. Blank it out. Take a deep breath. What's coming up?
CL: I wanted my daddy then too.

> Use of the word, "daddy" again indicates continued loss of adult observer position.

PM: Uh-huh.
CL: And I got mad at him. "Why are you being so mean to my mom?" And then, adult perspective, knowing that he was hurt himself.

> Although the "he was hurt himself" comment is a kind of very adult insight, it does not seem to flow out of the processing that has been done so far, so it seems to represent a disconnection from the target. We want the client to be connected to both the past event and the adaptive adult perspective.

PM: So, are you still here, with me, in this room?

> I am assessing the client's present awareness. (Checking for dissociation.) In this case the client says she is present, but probably is not. This would be a situation where another method of evaluation of the client's level of presence, like Jim Knipe's "Back of the Head Scale," would be more effective. (Knipe, 2009a)

CL: Yes.
PM: Just notice that. <><>

CL (laughs)
PM: Blank it out, and take a deep breath. What's coming up now?
CL: Everybody here is nice. (laughs) It's okay.

> She is apparently identifying with the child. The client's adult self is not sufficiently present.

PM: Just think of that. <><> Blank it out, and take a deep breath. What's coming up?
CL: I'm trying to just get rid of the hyperventilation feelings from crying, so I'm just going to take a little [inaudible]
PM: So on a scale of 0-10, with this memory, how disturbing is it for you now?
CL: I think it's still…a seven.

> Child identification and loss of adult perspective is probably responsible for lack of shift in SUDS.

PM: Were you laughing because you were going to disappoint me?
CL: Yes.
PM: Well, I'm totally okay with it being a seven, (laughs) I mean, I want to relieve you of the pain, but it's not for me, it's for you. So when you think about it being a seven, what stands out for you now?
CL: Being alone.
PM: Just notice that. <><> Try to keep your head still; just follow with your eyes.
CL: Oh, yeah. Sorry. (Laughs)
PM: <><> Now blank it out, and take a deep breath.
CL: I went to a safe place.

> Therapist is confused why the client would go to a safe place when no fear has been reported. Probably she is afraid of her overwhelming pain.

PM: Uh-huh. So tell me why you did that.
CL: That feeling of being alone was too scary I guess. I guess I needed to go there for a little bit.

Inadequate Preparation 145

> While avoidance is generally not a good thing during processing, in this case the client's autonomous choice to go to her safe place probably is positive because it represents a reduction of her need to please me and additional focus on what she wants for herself. It reassures her that she need not fear feeling overwhelmed, because she can return to her safe place.

PM: Ok. So, what's good about sitting here with me in this room, now?

> This intervention was introduced by Jim Knipe in his discussion of Continuous Installation of Positive Orientation and Safety (CIPOS). It is particularly helpful when the client seems to be losing connection to the present, including a present sense of safety. (Knipe, 2009a)

CL: What's good about it?
PM: Yeah.
CL: (laughs) Ok, I'm not alone. Would be an adult perspective. (Laughs) And we're going to get through this.
PM: Just think about that, alright?
CL: Okay.
PM: <><> Just notice. Just notice. That's right. That's good. Just notice. Just notice. That's right. That's good. Just notice. Good. Blank it out, and take a deep breath. What's coming up?
CL: Well, that's why it was so hard to come here in the first place. Coming alone, and coming to some place I've never been to before. Having to finagle everything from the BART to taxis to being in the wrong campus to everything. It was wrong. I was all alone.

> Popping out of the memory into current life usually indicates the client has lost touch with disturbance related to the target memory. This can happen when the target is resolved, which is not the case here, or when the client has cut off her emotional connection to the target memory. In addition, "alone" was not

> previously identified during the processing phase as central to the target memory. This appears to be a digression because the memory is overwhelming.

PM: So, go back to the memory now. And how disturbing is it now, on a scale of 0-10.
CL: Three, two, four, three. (Laughs)

> It is unclear how much processing has occurred. The lower SUDS may simply reflect that the client has disconnected from the memory.

PM: So what stands out now?
CL: That I'm here, and I'm okay.
PM: Just think about that. <><> Just notice. Just notice. Just notice. That's right. Just notice. That's right. That's good. That's good. Good. Just notice. That's right. That's right. Good. Good. That's right. Good. That's right. Good. Good. Just notice. Just notice. That's right. That's right. Good. Now blank it out, and take a deep breath. What's coming up now?
CL: My siblings aren't okay. But they're okay, they're adults, they went on. So I was going back and forth between "they're not ok," to "They're ok. They're ok. It's their own stuff. They've got to take care of their own stuff. I don't need to be responsible for that." Me feeling like they're not okay.

> The client seems to be addressing the responsibility distortion that causes her to feel she needs to take care of everybody, even at three years old. She is, however, talking about it in the context of their present "adult" lives, so she is disconnected from the original target, and simply intellectualizing about that situation. This is a good time to go back to target and try to restore an affective connection.

Inadequate Preparation

PM: So go back to the memory now. How disturbing is it now on a scale of 0-10.
CL: Which memory? Sorry.

> More indication that the client is disconnected from the target.

PM: This memory of sitting on the steps and hearing the sound.
CL: I guess a seven.

> Apparently, the client has reconnected to the memory and its accompanying disturbance.

PM: What's standing out that makes it a seven? What's disturbing?
CL: I can reach out and feel their pajamas. Like I have my hands on them, but I can't help anything.

> Confirmation of connection with the target experience of being there on the steps, but, again, loss of adult observer position. The disturbance is again her inability to help anyone.

PM: Just focus on that. <><> Blank it out, and take a deep breath. What's coming up?
CL: Of course they weren't okay. I wasn't okay. I was just little.

> Again addressing the inappropriateness of her three-year-old self feeling responsible for helping everyone. This time there seems to be a reasonable balance of child and adult perspective.

PM: Just think about that. <><> Blank it out, and take a deep breath. What's coming up now?
CL: Someone should've taken care of us. Someone should've been there. I deserved to be taken care of. I should've been taken care of. There should've been someone there.

This seems to represent productive adult perspective applied to the childhood experience. The repetition that the child should have been taken care of indicates to me the "newness" of that thought, and says to me that she is still connected to the child's experience while also in an adult observer role. This balance should lead to productive processing. .My experience is that it sometimes takes only a few sets of focused processing, in which the client is simultaneously holding the heart of the disturbing memory and an adaptive adult awareness, for a memory to substantially resolve. So, I consider even a short period of focused processing important.

PM: Just think of that. <><> Blank it out, and take a deep breath. What's coming up now?
CL: I'm really tired, and I just want to stop. (Laughs)

Why this comment arises at this particular time is interesting. My assumption is that it is a response to her discomfort with this very appropriate balance she has struck between child and adult perspective. This is really the first time in the session that she has done this effectively. At the risk of being overly analytical, I would suggest that it represents an activation of her independent autonomous adult self, which we have seen earlier is unfamiliar and difficult for her. (Recall the time earlier when she tried to focus her attention on pleasing me rather than addressing her internal issues.) Based on her response immediately after doing it, this show of autonomy is also threatening or scary for her. Children whose development of autonomy is discouraged at a very early age tend to expect criticism, attack or rejection if they show autonomous adult behavior. On a more basic level she has just criticized her parents in saying, "I should've been taken care of," a form of autonomous behavior which would have been sure to draw fire from her parents. I have seen many examples during practicums of clients asking to "stop" and therapists immediately complying without first trying to understand the source of the client's request. The reasonable response for the therapist is to find out what is coming up with the client that makes her want to stop.

PM: You want to stop this process? (Client nods.) Tell me what happened that made you come to that thought.
CL: I think I'm just becoming aware that it's taking a while. It's getting close to lunch and probably everyone is hungry and needs to take a break too.

The client is now feeling a need to take care of her fellow class members. Continuing with the hypothesis I just laid out, she is probably afraid of attack or retribution for showing her autonomous adult self, so, just when she becomes aware that "I should've been taken care of," she shifts to taking care of everyone else's needs. She turns her attention away from herself and her own needs towards those of the others in the room.

PM: So what you're saying is, "I want to stop, because I don't want to make people unhappy."
CL: Okay, yeah. Yeah. (Laughs)

The reality of the training situation is that, if the demo occurs before lunch, people are hungry, and the demo needs to be kept within a reasonable time frame, but the timing of her decision to stop and address this is, I believe, most important in this situation.

PM: That's reasonable. A reasonable consideration. How about if we just give it say four or five more minutes. Is that okay with you?
CL: Is that okay with everybody? (Laughs) (Class indicates "yes") Ok.
PM: Now what just came up?
CL: It was nice of them.
PM: Just think of that. <><> Blank it out and take a deep breath. Tell me what's coming up now.
CL: Probably just multiple other memories of not being taken care of.

> This seems to be an example of loss of the target memory, and floating to other memories, which I assume were later in time than 3 years old, the age of the client when the target memory occurred. The loss of connection to the target was probably a result of the minute or so of interruption about lunch that just occurred, and of her reaction to the threatening nature of the exploration she had just been doing. I respond by attempting to refocus her on the target.

PM: So what about this memory; how disturbing is it now on a scale of 0-10?
CL: Probably one or two.

> Despite the brief connection she made to a proper attribution of responsibility in recognizing that it should have been her parents rather than she who were in charge of taking care of everyone, this huge drop in disturbance seems suspect. There is no apparent reason for the SUDS to have dropped to this extent except loss of connection with the target memory, probably because of the interruption, the lack of remaining time in the session, and the threatening nature of her new adult perspective.

PM: What remains disturbing about it?
CL: I think where I went yesterday; wanting to be rescued.
PM: What's disturbing is wanting to be rescued?
CL: No. I guess that being alone, but I'm not alone. I guess that responsibility feeling, I don't know.

> The client wants to stop. She may be feeling her own low sugar levels before lunch. She may be feeling uncomfortable with the "responsibility feeling" she took on a few moments earlier. Having asked her to hang in 4 or 5 more minutes, I also want to wrap it up and close down the session.

Inadequate Preparation   151

PM: So it's the aloneness and there's responsibility. It's a one or a two. Do you have children that you're connected with? (Client nods) What ages are they?
CL: 28 through 17.
PM: So these are your children?
CL: Yeah.
PM: Yeah. So, think of one of them, perhaps that you feel closest to, and think of them at three years old. Can you do that?
CL: Ok.
PM: And imagine that they're in a situation like this, and they're feeling responsible, like they're supposed to protect their siblings and feeling alone. And you could be there as a spirit, as a nurturer. How would you help them feel better?

> This is a standard cognitive interweave for distortions in the area of responsibility. Sometimes an effective cognitive interweave is the fastest way to bring SUDS down in order to close down a session. Since the client did briefly make the necessary cognitive shift in an appropriate attribution of responsibility, the hope is that this intervention might remind her of that shift and secure the new adaptive adult perspective.

CL: There wasn't anything that I would've expected from any of them to be able to have made a difference for each other.
PM: So you'd let her know that it's not her responsibility,-that she's too small, and that she's doing what she can.
CL: Yeah.
PM: Just imagine you telling her that.
CL: Okay.
PM: <><> Blank it out, and take a deep breath. What's coming up now?
CL: That it's okay.
PM: It's okay. What does that mean?
CL: (laughs) Back to wanting this to be done. I'm sorry.

PM: That's fine. Stay with this just a minute or so (Client speaking over him: "Okay") and then I want to wrap it up.

But I do also want to know, "Is it disturbing? How disturbing is it? What, in fact, is disturbing?" This report of a low SUDS level seems suspect. Fortunately there is a practicum coming up after lunch that will permit further processing.

CL: It was a little bit difficult, because then I started going back to their childhoods and my parenting of them, and those mistakes.

> Again, loss of connection to the target.

PM: I see. So maybe it's better if you think of yourself as an adult to your own child, yourself...just that three-year-old you.
CL: Yeah.
PM: So just imagine helping her. Perhaps you want to put your arm around her. Just let her know.
CL: Okay.
PM: <><> Tell me what's coming up now?
CL: Is it okay that I picked her up?

> This is another autonomous action she has taken on her own without permission, and indicates she has again connected to the target memory.

PM: Yes.
CL: Ok. I picked her up, and took her into bed, and tucked her in. Tucked the blankets around her, and soothed her to sleep.

> This may represent a rescue or a caring adult perspective feeling compassion for the child. Either way, it seems useful, occurring as it does at the end of this session. If a rescue, it is an effective way to temporarily reduce the disturbance level to one appropriate for ending the session. If a caring adult perspective, it still

Inadequate Preparation 153

> accomplishes the desired result of lowering the disturbance level for ending the session. The question I had originally asked her is how she could "make the child feel better." Had we reached this point earlier in the session, the question, "how would you help her to feel better about herself" would have prevented a rescue response that would have been unwelcome at that stage of the session.

PM: So what's the message that you want her to hear, because you know that she feels powerless, responsible, and insignificant? So what is it that you want her to know?
CL: "Sweet baby. It's alright. It's over with now. It's ok. It's ok. You didn't cause this."
PM: Just think about telling her this. And see what her response is. <><> Blank it out, and take a deep breath. Tell me what's coming up now.
CL: I feel better.
PM: How disturbing is the memory?
CL: Zero.

> This SUDS report may be an effort to bring the session to a close. On the other hand, her last comments to her child self had a feeling of genuineness and spontaneity to them, and could have resulted in a further drop in SUDS, not necessarily to zero. In follow-up four months later she reported a positive result to the session, suggesting that a significant degree of resolution may have occurred.

PM: And what about the thought that, "I am significant, and I can make a difference." How true is that now on a scale of 1-7 where 7 is completely true and 1 is completely false. As you think of that memory, how true does it feel now on a gut level?
CL: Four or five.

PM: And is there another statement that would be better, more appropriate? I'm thinking perhaps, "I'm a competent adult." Does that feel more true now, than it felt when we started?
CL: Feel more true, right? Feel? (PM nods) Yeah.
PM: And how true does it feel on a scale of 1-7, when you think of this memory. "I'm a competent adult."
CL: Five or six.
PM: Ok. So I want you to think of that statement, "I'm a competent adult," and the memory, whatever form it is in now. Let me know when you have both.
CL: Ok.
PM: Just follow the wand <><> What's coming up now?

> According to the EMDR protocol, the Validity of Cognition should be a 6 or higher before proceeding to installation. In this case, an installation-like process is being used to help close down the session, which one would assume is incomplete.

CL: Just to remember that not many people can handle everything, and I do.
PM: Uh-huh. So you're recognizing how accomplished you are. (Client nods) Just think of that. <><> What's coming up?
CL: (laughs) I haven't really had fear of doing this in class, because I'm going to go back to Minnesota. (Laughs) Unless you come to Minnesota. Oh, funny!
PM: So I think that's a good place to stop. So everybody can go to lunch.
CL: Yeah, we can take care of them. (Laughs) Competent adults.
PM: Okay, good. Thank you for doing this.
CL: Thank you

Four month follow-up:
"I did continue back at home to do more processing of still other memories related to that primary one that day. I believe it is resolved."

7

Getting the Right Floatback

(Video #7 in JFKU site)

In this session, there was some confusion on the client's part of what the actual target was, and there was some difficulty staying with it. I was able to keep the target in focus, although I lost clarity at one point. Given that, the session is a testimony to the resilience of the EMDR protocol in that the issue did process successfully, and remained resolved at follow-up. (34 Minutes)

PM: So, do you have a target? Do you have an issue?
CL: Do I have an issue? Yes. Sometimes I think that my family doesn't take me seriously.
PM: And your family consists of your…?
CL: I have a husband and three sons, all grown.
PM: And what does not taking you seriously mean?
CL: Well, they don't necessarily think that my profession is that serious. They don't think… when we're all giving opinions about something, they sort of gloss over (and say) "That's really nice mom" or "Well okay honey." Kind of pat pat thing.
PM: Okay. And this is painful for you?
CL: Yes.

PM: On a scale of 0 to 10, how painful would you say it is when they do this?
CL: Eight.
PM: Okay. And do they know that it's painful?
CL: I think that they do, but I think that they also just think that just a little pat or a little "It's okay mom, we take you as seriously as we take our professions." I think that they think that that's enough and then it happens again. It's reoccurring and that's the problem. It's not that it's a onetime thing, it's reoccurring.

> As a rule of thumb, when an upset is recurring, it is clearly being fed by an earlier feeder memory. If it weren't for the residual response pattern coming from the earlier trauma, she would not have been triggered in the present, and she would have found a way to either effectively resolve the current behavior or not take it personally.

PM: Do you feel like they're condescending to you?
CL: Yes, not in a mean way. But it's like "I'm a mechanical engineer" or "I'm an accountant" or "I'm a lawyer, so that's real work".
PM: So, what emotions come up? Did this happen recently? Last night, maybe?

> The client was so activated, that I assumed the issue had come up in the previous 24 hours. She seems to be angry.

CL: Yes.
PM: So is that the best example, last night, or is there another?
CL: Yes, and no.
PM: So when you think of what happened last night, do you have an image?
CL: Yes.
PM: And what do you feel?
CL: Hurt.

Getting the Right Footback 157

PM: And when you think of the image, and you feel the hurt, what do you feel in your body?
CL: Tightness around my mouth and my jaw. You can kind of see that I start to bite my lip so I don't say anything.

> Tension around the jaw is usually related to anger. It is like a child who wants to show his or her anger by biting, but is restraining that impulse by clamping her mouth shut, resulting in jaw tension. An older child might want to verbally protest but clamps the mouth closed out of fear, guilt or shame.

PM: Anyplace else?
CL: Sometimes up here in the temples.
PM: But not now.

> When a client says "sometimes," "usually," "probably" or switches to past tense, they are not reporting a present experience.

CL: Just a little bit, but mostly around my mouth right now.
PM: And the feelings in your temples, and the feeling in your jaw, they have to do with hurt?
CL: Yes. It's kind of like I can't say anything I have to just take it. Hide the hurt.
PM: Uh-huh. You look sad now.
CL: Yeah, I feel very sad.
PM: And where do you feel the sadness?
CL: Behind my eyes.
PM: So as you feel that sadness, the feeling behind your eyes, and the feeling in your jaw, and perhaps your temples, can you feel that now?
CL: Uh-huh.
PM: So let your mind float back to an early memory.

> To me, a float back is a simple process that seems to be commonly distorted and made ineffective. I keep the instruction as short and simple as possible. I make sure the client is in touch

with the physical sensations, and then I say, "Good, let your mind float back to an early memory." The shorter the instruction, the less likely it is to stimulate left-brain activity. I believe that floatback should be a right-brain process that enables both explicit and implicit memories to emerge.

CL: Okay.
PM: What are you noticing? What's coming up?
CL: A picture of my mom saying essentially the same thing, "Oh, Nancy!"
PM: At what age?
CL: Nine.
PM: That's pretty specific, are you thinking of an event?
CL: Yes, I was the oldest child of five and I was taking care of my siblings, and my younger siblings *tell* my mother that I'm not taking good care of them and I *try* to explain what happened and my mother says "Oh, Nancy!" So again, just not taken very seriously.

The use of present tense in describing this event indicates the client has good access to the experience of that memory. Normally I look for the client to indicate visual accessing by moving her eyes up and to the right or left. (Neuro-Linguistic Programming (NLP) accessing cues are discussed in Chapter One.) When I see that movement, I infer she is looking at an image. In this case she repeatedly imitates what is apparently her mother's gesture of dismissal, from which I assumed she was seeing her mother's face. More precisely, I could have said, "So you're seeing that gesture?"

PM: So you're seeing her face?
CL: Yes, my mother's face, in kind of like physical motion.
PM: And how disturbing is that memory?
CL: Six.

Getting the Right Foatback 159

PM: Six. What's confusing for me is that that's a memory of being kind of dismissed. Not that you're not important that or what you're doing is not important. Just kind of "stop complaining"
CL: Most of the time growing up I felt kind of dismissed by my mother. So, I don't know, but that's the picture that came up.
PM: So, is that the way you feel with your husband and your sons.
CL: Yes
PM: You feel dismissed?
CL: Yes
PM: So it has to do with your concerns. Well, it's that your job is not important, but with your mother your concerns are not important.
CL: Right.
PM: You have the same physical sensation when you think of your mother?
CL: Yup.

> After a floatback, it is necessary to verify that the memory that came up is indeed a feeder for the memory you started with. The physical sensation should be the same (because that's what you floated back on), the emotion, the level of activation, and probably the cognitive distortion, which eventually becomes the Negative Cognition.

PM: Okay. So, bring up that image of your mother's face.
CL: Okay.
PM: You've got it?
CL: Yes.
PM: And what's the negative thought that comes to mind about yourself now?
CL: Inadequate.
PM: Inadequate?
CL: Yeah.
PM: I'm inadequate?
CL: Inadequate.

PM: So, what would you prefer to believe about yourself, now, when you think of that image of your mother's face?
CL: I'm adequate, I'm good enough. I'm good.
PM: I'm good. I'm good enough. So on a scale of 1 to 7, where seven is completely true and one is completely false, when you think of that image of your mother's face, on a gut level, how true does that statement feel now, "I'm good enough."
CL: Two.
PM: And, you were feeling sad. Are you still feeling sad?
CL: Yeah, I still feel very sad. I still feel very hurt.
PM: Hurt, anything else?
CL: The word that comes to my mind is invisible.
PM: Invisible. Any possibility that there's also some anger or irritation?
CL: I was never allowed to be angry with my mother so I never felt anger.
PM: Yes, but we're talking about here and now.
CL: I still struggle to feel any anger.
PM: Yeah.
CL: Probably some anger. Probably more irritation.
PM: So, you said it was a 6 before on a scale of 0 to 10. How disturbing is it for you now?
CL: Eight.

> If the assessment phase is effective, the level of disturbance often goes up.

PM: And where are you feeling the disturbance now in your body?
CL: I still feel it in my mouth and my face, but I also feel it in my gut.
PM: So, I want you to focus on the feeling in your mouth, your face, your gut. The thought, "I'm inadequate," and the image of your mother's face. Tell me when you've got all that.

> I seem to be repeating this over and over because it is so important, the therapist must bring all the elements of the target

Getting the Right Foatback   161

moment together and specifically reference each one, and then wait until the client has brought it all together. Only then should BLS begin.

CL: Okay.
PM: Ok. Just follow the wand. And just notice what's coming up. <><> Just notice. Just notice. That's right, just notice. Good. Just notice. Just notice. That's right, just notice. That's good. Just notice, good. Good. Good. That's right, that's good. Good. Good. Now blank it out. Take a deep breath, what's coming up now?
CL: I have a picture of my mother walking away from the dresser drawer, closing the dresser drawer and walking away.

> This comment was confusing. It did not seem to relate to the memory that was the target. If it was a new memory, I thought it odd that the client did not acknowledge that she was talking about something I did not know about. I was not sure if it was a fantasy that came to her mind or an actual memory.

PM: So is that something that occurred?
CL: I don't know. I was an infant
PM: Oh you're talking about a time when you were an infant?
CL: My mother...When I was born, I weighed 4 pounds, and my mother put me in the dresser drawer as a bassinet.
PM: So this is an image you have, that you've been told about?
CL: Yes.
PM: So just focus on that. <><> Blank it out and take a deep breath. What's coming up for you now?
CL: I feel very shaky.

> I felt like I was skating on thin ice here. We had started with a well-defined target, and now the client is referencing an event that she does not actually remember, but has been told about. Normally I would think that this memory could not be a feeder because the client was told about it and it would not have had

strong SUDS, but she is now reporting that she feels shaky, and physiological responses to new material usually indicate that the client is accessing the material strongly.

PM: You're shaking?
CL: Mm-hm.
PM: Is that related to this last image?
CL: Yes.
PM: Or to your mother's face? Let me just ask you a question or two. How did you pick the nine-year-old age originally? What made you pick nine?

I am now trying to sort out the meaning and significance of the two events, the nine-year-old one and the new one that was just reported involving being a newborn.

CL: That was the first time I can remember my mother actually saying something to me that felt dismissive. Like I wasn't important, I was invisible. It didn't matter what I...
PM: Yes, and this memory of your mother walking away from the dresser, what's the relationship between that and what we started with, the nine-year-old memory?

The relationship is clear, but it felt to me like apples and oranges. The nine-year-old event is something that actually happened, the memory of which evokes disturbing feeling in the client. The dresser drawer story is a fantasy that, although it could be evocative of disturbing feeling, seems flatter, less multi-dimensional.

CL: That I was always dismissed. That I was, I was pretty much invisible, maybe unwanted. But it was never said, until I was, I don't remember. The first time I remember was around nine, and then I remember thinking about the dresser drawer that somebody had said, my mother had said when I was nine that they used to put me in the dresser drawer because I was so small.

> Note that the part about her mother closing the drawer with the client in it and walking away was not part of what she had been told. So this fantasy image is a metaphor for the way the client perceives herself to have been treated by her mother. In my view an actual memory is much better as a target than a metaphor which, during processing, can evolve into a more elaborate metaphor or a series of other metaphors, without necessarily getting to the intensely painful affect of the target.

CL: And so I think that it just feels like that was a bad thing. That when my mother was being dismissive and talking to me and dismissing me at (age) nine, that I thought back to that and was kind of like, well it's always been that way. It's always been dismissive. It's just that this is the first time she's really, you know, said that you're not that important, that you're invisible, that, you know, "Oh, Nancy!" Kind of like…

> I decide to stay with the nine-year-old memory, because it was well defined, vivid, and was described by the client as a "first."

PM: And how disturbing is this memory from nine-years-old now?
CL: Seven.
PM: And what stands out about it, what makes it disturbing?

> When a therapist or client loses the thread of a target, it is useful to go back to the target and ask, "What stands out now as disturbing?" If the target has lost a lot of its activation because of the interruption, it may be necessary to remind the client of the emotionally triggering components of the target.

CL: It makes it disturbing because it felt like, that my mother was always... she never...I was never important, but I didn't realize... I never felt unimportant until she was being dismissive in that instance.

> At this point, I was thinking I had made a mistake in the assessment phase. If I have any doubt about whether a client is describing her experience at the time the event occurred or her experience when she is recalling it in the room with me, I ask. Similarly, if I have any doubt about whether the negative cognition is about the client in the present or simply a description of the situation in the past event, I ask. When the target event occurred, this client was mostly angry about receiving those messages from her mother, husband and sons. Anger is generally a secondary emotion when it appears initially in a target, and it is often an indication of externalization, which is a defensive focusing on other people and situations rather than feeling vulnerable feelings like hurt, helplessness, or fear. In addition to the appearance of anger in her tight clenched jaw, however, this client seemed to also have a look of hurt expressed in her moist eyes.

PM: So when you think about her being dismissive, what stands out about that experience, about that event, that scene?
CL: The nine-year-old or the...
PM: Nine-year-old.
CL: She's kind of the same thing, not closing the drawer but sort of "Oh, Nancy" pushing me out of the way, pushing me back, pushing me...

> Client makes a repeated gesture with her arm of her mother pushing her away. Spontaneous gestures are often powerful gateways into a target. In this case the client's gesture seems to represent both a visual and a visceral sense of being pushed away.

PM: You actually see her making this motion of pushing you away?
CL: Yes.

Getting the Right Footback 165

PM: Can you focus on that?

CL: Yes.

PM: <><> Just notice what's coming up, just notice. Just notice. Just notice, that's right. That's good. That's good. Good. And blank it out, and take a deep breath. What stands out now?

> "Just notice what's coming up, just notice. Just notice. Just notice, that's right. That's good. That's good. Good" are "cadence comments." The purpose of these comments is to help keep the client connected to the therapist as a resource, reduce performance anxiety connected to the EMDR process itself, and maintain the client's tie to the present, her adult non-dissociated self. The term "cadence comments" has the somewhat dubious distinction of being the only phrase I have ever "googled" to which I have not found a single direct reference. My best guess is that the term was coined by Francine Shapiro. It was included in the EMDR Basic Training during the early nineties before the Basic Principles and Protocols book (Shapiro, 1995, 2001) was written, and, to the best of my recollection, Shapiro used cadence comments in every demo video of her conducting EMDR that was shown in the trainings. In the mid-nineties, the Institute began showing a video of Dr. Robert Tinker working with an elderly woman whose husband had left her when he found out she had terminal cancer. In this video as well, cadence comments played a prominent role. There is, however, no reference to "cadence comments" in the index of Dr. Shapiro's seminal text (Shapiro, 1995, 2001), and over the years the term seems to have disappeared from the Institute trainings, so that when I mentioned it in a recent meeting of EMDRIA-approved trainers, half of the trainers had never heard it before. Guidelines for using cadence comments are discussed more fully in Chapter One of this volume.

CL: I can just see... I can still see my mother's face.

> There is, at this point a definite reduction in the tension in her jaw that seemed previously to represent where her anger was held. In

fact, at this point, her mouth is a little open so that her jaw is clearly not clenched. The dominant feeling here seems to be hurt.

PM: Stay with that <><> Just notice. That's right, that's good. Just notice. That's right, that's good. Just notice. That's right. Good, good, good, good. Now, blank it out and take a deep breath. What's coming up now?
CL: I have a lot less tension in my temples and my mouth. I feel less shaky.

These seem to be indications that processing is occurring.

PM: Just notice the difference.

This is an instruction I learned from Jim Knipe when we were observing each other work with Turkish earthquake victims after the 1999 earthquake in Turkey. I like it because the instruction requires the client to think of her state of being before the change and the state she is in now. Presumably the client cannot really bring back her experience from before the change, because it has changed. Realizing how difficult it is to think about the pre-change state helps make the client solidly aware that there has been change. If the change is not stable and the client is able to recall the pre-change state, thinking of the difference can make the change more solid.

<><>
CL: I'm sorry.
PM: What's happening? You had trouble tracking physically?
CL: Yes.
PM: Oh you said to me before we started that you have trouble with fast eye movements?
CL: Yes.
PM: And what did you say?

CL: Just that I had trouble tracking. I had trouble tracking with the wand. Usually they just tap.
PM: I see. Are we doing okay with your eyes right now?
CL: Yeah, yeah.

> When clients have trouble tracking I make adjustments in the eye movements before abandoning them in favor of another form of BLS. Research indicates that eye movements are superior, especially with intrusive images, and I find that slowing down the eye movements is usually sufficient to make the client comfortable with visual tracking.

PM: Good, tell me what's coming up now?
CL: Well, it's almost like I see this picture of me, kind of, with my hands on my hips saying, "No. That's not true. That, that's not true. This is wrong. This is wrong. This is not true."

> One way of interpreting this comment is that it supports the possibility I mentioned earlier that the client was not aware she had internalized the message that she was not important, and she is angry at her mother for that suggestion. Typically anger, when it comes up in the initial discussion of a target, represents the adult's current point of view. The child was usually not angry at the time, but was instead hurt, ashamed or afraid. Now, the adult looks back and is angry, and then projects that anger onto the child. It is the adult who has the anger, but in that case the anger is serving a defensive role to keep the adult from accessing the child's vulnerable feelings.
>
> In hindsight, however, I now question whether I understood the core issue in this target. I believe now that the client's last comment represented her struggle with her inability to express her anger at her mother, with whom anger is "not allowed." I assume the same is true for her present family. So, in her fantasy, she is standing up to her mother, and expressing her anger. The hurt of her mother's demeaning attitude towards her was not new to this

target event. What was new was the explicitness of it. The hurt would have more to do with earlier incidents in which mom's demeaning attitude was implicit. In those events, she would have been younger and presumably would not have had sufficient distance from the message to be angry about it. The core issue in this particular event, however, seems to be the client's anger and indignation at her mother when her mother explicitly voices the dismissive message.

PM: So that's an annoyed little girl?
CL: Uh-huh. Yeah, well, almost angry with my mother, which is not allowed. But somehow asserting myself, and saying, "No this is wrong."
PM: And where do you feel that in your body?
CL: I feel it right here in my side.

> In early trainings and subsequent remarks, Dr. Shapiro has recommended locating the associated body sensation whenever a new emotion emerges. In this case I was asking about the physical sensation to help ground the client in her present experience

PM: Just notice that. <><> Blank it out and take a deep breath. What are you noticing now?
CL: Just a lot of sadness. A lot of sadness. A lot of sadness for myself, and a lot of sadness for my mother.

> This comment seems to represent movement past the anger towards the child's more vulnerable feelings, although it is unclear if the client is accessing the child's sadness or observing it.

PM: Just focus on that. <><> Blank it out and take a deep breath. What's coming up now?
CL: I see myself as an adult, and I see my sons and my husband all standing behind my mother.

> The client is assuming an adult position in which she is recognizing that her attitude toward her family mirrors her attitude towards her mom. I was unclear at this point whether the anger was central to this target or whether she was avoiding more vulnerable feelings by focusing on the anger. I decided to return to the target and see if the target had shifted at all. If it had, we might be able to use that shift as a way to access the vulnerable feelings that have become partially resolved. In hindsight, I believe that the need for the client to access the vulnerable feelings was not coming so much from the client as it was from my misreading the central issue in this target.

PM: So when you think of that original memory, from nine years old, how disturbing is that now? On a scale of 0 to 10?
CL: Four.
PM: Four, and what is still disturbing?
CL: That people would be dismissive, that people would - family members think that what I do is less important than what they do.
PM: You're talking about currently now, right?

> I need to keep the client focused on the past event. Focusing on the present situation confuses the processing and does not lead to resolution unless it comes at a time when the initial target is essentially resolved.

CL: I'm talking about... yes, but I see myself talking to my mother, but my mother is the age that she was when I was nine. But my husband and my sons are the current age.
PM: I want to see if we can focus for now on that old memory and leave your sons and your husband for after we process this piece.
CL: Okay.
PM: And thinking back to that memory from four years old...
CL: Nine years old?
PM: I'm sorry, nine years old. What stands out now?

CL: That I'm standing as an adult, standing behind my nine-year-old self and just saying "No this isn't right, this isn't true".
PM: Just imagine that. <><> Blank it out and take a deep breath. What are you noticing now?
CL: Everyone in the room is gone but me.
PM: Me the nine-year-old or me the adult?
CL: Me the adult.
PM: Everyone in the room is gone? Your mother and the nine-year-old are gone?
CL: Yes.

> I wasn't sure what this represented, but I did not think originally it was a productive association. When I question whether a client is processing productively or in defense, as I was with this client, I evaluate every comment the client makes to determine if it appears to represent progress in processing or defense. I decided to go back to the target in the hopes of picking up the remaining activation. When I consider now that the client did not feel safe talking back to her mother or her husband and sons, and I wonder if this wasn't the central issue in this memory, I think the distortion (NC) must have been in the area of safety. Safety issues usually resolve as the client becomes aware that, with the passage of time, the danger has passed. Her seeing everyone else disappear from the room, and her being adult and alone, may have represented an awareness that she is now an adult and she is safe.

PM: Huh. So when you think of that memory, how disturbing is that now on a scale 0 to 10, where zero is not disturbing and ten is the worst you can imagine?
CL: One.
PM: It's a one? And what makes it a one? What's still disturbing?
CL: Just I can feel still some tightness in my face. I just feel still a little tight, some residual I think.
PM: And that tightness has to do with the anger?
CL: Yes, yes absolutely.

PM: Can you imagine your mother there, and you actually becoming angry at her and telling her what you think?

> Shapiro suggests, in the section of her book on cognitive interweaves, asking the client to express forbidden feelings. The client has mentioned that she was not allowed to express anger, and she seems to have been feeling anger throughout this session. I think if I had gotten the negative cognition right, it would have had more to do with not having a right, perhaps to defend herself or to demand respect. As a negative cognition, these would capture the client's present belief about herself in relation to her family, as well as her original experience with her mother. In this intervention, I am actually suggesting that the client do the thing she has been struggling with, express the feelings that have been forbidden.

CL: I can try. (Laughs)
PM: Nobody's going to…There's no retribution here. She's not here. <><> Just notice. That's right. That's right, that's good, good, good, good. Just notice. That's right, that's good. You're doing great. Just notice. That's right. That's right, good, good, good. Blank it out now and take a deep breath. And what's coming up now?
CL: I'm laughing and saying to my mom, "This is ridiculous what you're thinking?"
PM: So, how disturbing is the memory now?
CL: Zero.
PM: Good. And what about the statement, "I'm good enough"? How true does that feel when you think of the memory?
CL: 10.
PM: 10? On a scale 1 to 7, it's a seven.
CL: 10, it's a 7, it's off the charts.

> If I had been following the EMDR protocol more accurately here, I would have asked her if "I'm good enough" was still in fact the best positive cognition, and perhaps we would have come up with

a better one, like "I have a right to respect" or "I have a right to express my feelings/anger."

PM: So, I want you to think of that statement, "I'm good, I'm good enough" and think about whatever form that original memory is in now.
CL: The original memory?
PM: From nine years old.
CL: Nine years old.
PM: And tell me when you've got them both.
CL: Okay
PM: Good. <><> Blank it out, take a deep breath. What's coming up?
CL: The words, "I'm important, I'm valuable, I'm good enough."
PM: Just think of that. <><> Blank it out and take a deep breath. What's coming up now?
CL: All the tension's gone from my face, and I don't feel it anymore in my gut.
PM: So scan your body, close your eyes, scan your body, and tell me if there's any disturbing sensation.
CL: Okay. There's a little bit behind my eyes, still behind my eyes.
PM: Just focus on that.
CL: Okay. <><>
PM: What are you noticing now?
CL: I feel fine. I feel good.
PM: The tension around your eyes is still there? Or gone?
CL: No, it's gone.
PM: Great. Well, I don't think you'll need to address this again, but if you do, you have a practicum after this.
CL: Good. Great. Thank you
PM: You're welcome.

> After the recorder was turned off I asked the client how disturbing the original incident was of her husband and sons not taking her work seriously. She said it was a zero.

8

Getting the Target Right

The transcripts in this volume illustrate many things, but most important to me is the critical role played by a clean assessment. Everything has to make sense to create the optimal conditions for EMDR processing. When I am presented with a target that is not resolving, very often the problem is with the formulation of the target. In consulting about a stalled target, I start with very basic questions: Where did the processing get stuck? Is there reason to think there might be a feeder memory? Is there a lightning rod moment? What is the image of the worst moment? What is the negative cognition? What is the dominant emotion? As each piece of the puzzle is put into place, I make sure it fits.

Getting the Target Right

EMDR is a robust protocol. As clinicians, we can make mistakes and get things wrong, and the target will often still resolve. My emphasis on getting the target right addresses the minority of targets that do not fully resolve. If there is a feeder memory that was not identified during the Assessment Phase, it may emerge during the Desensitization and Reprocessing Phase, but it may not. If not, the processing session will be incomplete or entirely unsuccessful. If the focus is intended to be an image that captures the worst moment, and it does not really address the worst part of the memory; or it is not really a moment in time; or it is not really an image but instead a video clip or a felt sense, the target might resolve and it might not. If it does not, I recommend reprocessing the target after fixing these problems. But the real message in this volume is to start with a clean congruent target in the first place that will make the processing phase move as efficiently as possible and will offer the best chance for success.

Lessons from Memory Reconsolidation Research

How important, for instance, is it to focus on a snapshot image rather than a video clip? It's only of critical importance if the avoidance of the worst moment ends up preventing successful processing. Getting a snapshot forces the client to identify a moment in time. We are asking her to think of the worst moment. A video clip may contain the worst moment, but thinking of the whole clip is an easy way to avoid focusing on that worst moment. Many targets that do not process successfully fail because the client does not fully access the core disturbance. As described in Chapter One, an important lesson learned from memory reconsolidation research is that **in order to resolve a traumatic memory, we must ring the bell.**

For instance, a client came to me with a disturbing memory from a successful surgery she had undergone six years back. Afterwards she had continued to have excessive fear of medical procedures. The memory had been processed once in a ninety minute EMDR session with another therapist, at the end of which she told the therapist that the disturbance had gone from a seven to a three. In fact it was still at a seven. She had reported a SUDS of three to the therapist because she did not want him to feel bad about the session. I asked her for the details of how the target was set up (the Assessment). She reported the emotion first, saying that she was still scared when she thought of the memory. The image she described was of being on the gurney, being wheeled out of a room down the hall and through the double doors of the operating room. This was a video clip, not a snapshot. I asked her for the image of the worst moment. After some false starts, she was surprised to realize that the snapshot of the worst part was her husband's scared look as she was being wheeled out of the room. When she now thought of that scared look, her disturbance shot up to ten, and she remembered feeling terrified. With this clarification of the target, it processed fully in ten minutes.

The other lesson from memory reconsolidation research is that the cognitive distortion associated with the traumatic event must be successfully challenged in order for the memory to become unlinked from the disturbing emotion. If we as clinicians do not help the client get the negative cognition and positive cognitions right, or if there are more than one, the client may figure it all out during BLS, or not. If not, the target will not resolve, and we will need to go back to the target memory and help them figure it out. Then we will need to process the target again with the proper cognitive pieces in place. In this volume, I am advocating getting it all right from the beginning, so that the chances for success are maximized, and targets will not need to be processed over and over to make up for previous unsuccessful processing sessions.

The Makings of a "Crisp" Target

In the first Chapter, I listed a variety of conditions that defined what I call a "crisp" target:
- The emotion fits with the image, and the intensity is appropriate.
- Negative cognition and emotions are congruent.
- Negative and positive cognitions are about the present. (Listen for past tense.)
- Positive and Negative cognitions are mutually congruent.
- Positive and Negative cognitions are consistent developmentally with the client's age at the time of the memory.
- Positive and Negative cognitions apply to presenting (triggering) event as well as earlier TARGET memory!
- Body sensations and emotions are congruent in location and intensity.

- SUDS level is congruent with description of the trauma, client's presentation, and words chosen to describe emotions.
- SUDS, NC and PC are all about the present, not the past, and are viscerally felt.
- The emotions and cognitions are consistent with the client's symptoms.

Hopefully, the transcripts in this volume have illustrated these points, but I believe this issue is of such great importance that some further examples might be helpful.

Congruent Cognitions

For instance, a case was presented to me of a middle-aged woman who was tortured by her brother as a young child. The negative cognition was "I can't get away." That cognition sounds like it is a description of what was true of the original target situation so it fails the test of a good cognition in two ways: it does not represent a distortion because it was true and it does not apply to the client in the present. Upon further exploration the cognition that seemed to make more sense was "I'm not important," a conclusion that she had drawn in childhood from her mother's unwillingness to protect her and that endures in present time to her adult self.

Another case involved a man who had received a critical evaluation at work and was unable to get out of bed for a week. His negative cognition was "I'm worthless." A floatback (somatic bridge) resulted in a memory from thirteen in which he had made a minor repair on his father's car and did not put all the parts back properly, so that a professional repair was necessitated. That memory was processed and went from a 6 to a 4. My take on the target is that "I'm worthless" seems to be a belief that would develop earlier in a boy's life than his teens. I suggested the therapist do another somatic bridge, which identified a memory form being four years old and his mother becoming extremely upset when, in an effort to help her, he broke a valued family heirloom.

Getting the Target Right 177

I sometimes work extensively with clients in exploring a target until it makes sense to me. In my experience, the worst moment in targets involving severe car accidents seem to almost always be when the client recognized that the impact was inevitable. Sometimes, the client has been terrified and feared for her life. Sometimes, she has feared for the life of her child in the back seat. Sometimes, the car was headed for a worse calamity as a result of the initial impact, and that memory is scarier than the initial impact. So if a client describes a car accident and tells me the worst part was realizing she had been driving too fast, I wonder about whether the she is avoiding the worst part, because she doesn't want to think about it. I will ask about that, so that the target will eventually make sense to me. If the memory is processed with EMDR and the client avoids thinking about the worst part, she might eventually focus on the worst part during BLS, or she might not. If not, the target will not fully process.

In my work with earthquake victims, I have found that their worst moment is almost always at the first sign of the earthquake. Often there is a sound just before the shaking begins, and that brings up fear. I don't require clients to identify that moment as the worst part, but if they don't, I will ask about it. In explaining why the chosen moment is indeed most painful, the client will sometimes provide additional information that makes everything make sense. If my attempts at understanding the target fail, I will go ahead and attempt to process it with the client, hoping that it will all fall into place during BLS.

A lot of time can be wasted processing aspects that are peripheral to a target memory or the wrong event entirely, while the client avoids the most intense part of the memory. Signs that this may be happening, in addition to the therapist's sense that what the client is describing as the worst part does not really make sense for what actually happened, might be a lack of congruent affect, or a negative or positive cognition that does not correlate with the symptoms that resulted from the event. For instance, after the car accident the client has been excessively fearful on the road, but the emotion she is reporting is guilt, or the negative cognition is "I'm irresponsible." When clients suggest a target involving dread, I want to know what happened that made them afraid. That will be the real target.

Congruent Emotions

In addition to a client's stated emotions being congruent with what she appears to be feeling, we also want the emotions to fit with what would be expected of the kind of event she is trying to resolve. Recently, I consulted on a case involving a client who was raped by her mother's boyfriend at an early age. Usually, I expect to hear that the client feels fear, guilt or disgust. This client, however, only reported feeling sad. The target had not resolved in two sessions of EMDR processing. If a target is not resolving, I am always asking myself, "What's wrong with this picture?" Why is sadness the only feeling being reported here? Where are the others? Upon further discussion with the client, she explained that she had felt disgust and confusion, but that the sadness was stronger, because she had told her mother about him touching her inappropriately and she had not taken action to protect her. After sorting it out, what became clear is that there were three targets to process. The first was the initial molestation, involving confusion and anger. The second was telling her mother and her mother's scolding her for flirting with the boyfriend, which involved primarily sadness and resentment. And the third was the rape, which involved fear, disgust, shame and anger. Once the targets were properly sorted out, they were processed in chronological order and resolved.

Sexual Molestation: Avoiding Projection

Whenever I hear about sexual molestation, I ask how intense a violation it was. I want to know how long it went on and whether the client told anyone about it. If not, why not? Of course, we gather this information while being careful to avoid implying in any way that the client did something wrong or was in some way culpable. We cannot assume we know the nature of the trauma, until we have the information. I have heard molestation referred to as a trauma of neglect. I believe it often is. If there was only a single instance, the victim probably had adults she could go to for protection who intervened. If it went on over time, usually she did not feel free to get help. The lack of available safe help is commonly a deeper problem, and suggests the likelihood of finding feeder memories related to neglect. If we approach the target with preconceived ideas about the nature of the trauma without verifying our assumptions with the client, we can end up not ringing the bell.

Fear is not always present in molestations. I have worked with men who were molested at a very young age without penetration who found it confusing, but interesting. Even though they may have been upset about it when recalling it from adulthood, the incident itself could have had no SUDS because they might have liked the perpetrator or enjoyed the attention. Although the incident might be very upsetting for the therapist to hear about, my experience is that it will not be a good EMDR target for the client if there was no disturbance at the time.

Sometimes the child consents to molestation because she is so starved for attention that the neglect is a more devastating alternative than being molested. There is almost always disgust and shame. Especially if the child became aroused sexually, there is confusion and shame about the possibility that she might have welcomed the molestation. My friend and colleague, Harriet Sage, MFT, developed a wonderful cognitive interweave to address this confusion: "If you had had a choice between being molested and feeling pleasure or being out with your friends playing, which would you have chosen?" Again, in these cases, the target will not have been fully processed until the neglect is addressed. In general, resolution of childhood issues where the cognitive distortion in the area of responsibility requires the adult client to feel compassion for the child. If molestation occurred largely as a result of neglect, and the client feels responsible for letting it happen over a period of years, it will be difficult for her to understand her actions and forgive herself until she has explored the issues around neglect so that she can feel compassion.

Conclusion

With the publication of this volume, I am thrilled to be able to make my work public, so that other clinicians can evaluate it and hopefully learn from it. This, the second of my books on clinical technique, joins the website being launched by JFK University with the videos of the sessions transcribed in both volumes and many more. (Video numbers are included at the beginning of each chapter to facilitate identifying the corresponding video on the University site.) By including examples of my work and the thinking that has gone into it in these projects, I have attempted to make my approach to EMDR transparent and accessible. What I am sharing is personal. It is a style that has evolved over decades that I find effective. Although natural to me, it may not be comfortable for everyone. I think there is a need for this level of sharing in the EMDR community. I hope that these contributions will become a model for future volumes by other clinicians presenting their own unique styles of conducting EMDR.

Readers interested in being notified when additional books or clinical DVDs by Dr. Manfield are available for distribution should email the publisher at EMDRUpClose@gmail.com. (Emails must contain the words "EMDR Up Close" in the subject or body.)

Until now, the video numbering that appears at the beginning of each chapter was independent of the numbering system used by JFK University in their video site, www.emdrclinicalvideos.com. With this printing, the Video numbers at the beginning of each chapter now correspond to the number being used in JFKU's website.

References

Ahsen, A, Basic Concepts in Eidetic Psychotherapy, Brandon House, Bronx, New York, 1973

Bandler, R. & J. Grinder *[- Frogs into Princes: Neuro Linguistic Programming].* Moab, UT: Real People Press. pp. 15,24,30,45,52.1979.

Bernstein E. and F. Putnam, "Development, reliability, and validity of a dissociation scale". *J. Nerv. Ment. Dis.* 174 (12): 727–35, 1986.

Black, C., *It's Never Too Late to Have a Happy Childhood,* MAC Publishing, Bainbridge Island, WA ,1989

Bouton, M.E. (2004) Context and Behavioral Processes in Extinction. Learning and Memory, 11, 485-494.

Bregman, N. J., & Mahan J. (1972). Cue-dependent amnesia in rats. Journal of Comparative and Physiological Psychology, 81, 243–247

Christman, S.D., Garvey, K.J., Propper, R.E. & Phaneuf, K.A., Bilateral eye movements enhance the retrieval of episodic memories. British Journal of Clinical Psychology, 40, 257-280, (in press).

Duvarci, S. & Nader, K.(2004) Characterization of Fear Memory Reconsolidation Journal of Neuroscience. 24, 9269-9275

Duvarci, S., Mamou, C.S. & Nadar, K. (2006), Extincton is not a sufficient condition to prevent fear memories from undergoing reconsolidation in the basolateral amygdale, European Journal of Neuroscience, 24, 249-260.

Erickson, M. and E. Rossi, "The February Man: Facilitating New Identity in Hypnotherapy" by Erickson and Rossi, The <u>Collected Papers of Milton H. Erickson on Hypnosis, Volume 4</u>, Ernest L. Rossi, Ed., Irvington Publishers, 1980.

Erickson, M. and E. Rossi, Experiencing Hypnosis: Therapeutic Approaches to Altered States, Irvington Publishers, 1981.

Hernandez, P. J., & Kelley, A. E. (2004). Long-term memory for instrumental responses does not undergo protein synthesis-dependent reconsolidation upon retrieval. Learning & Memory, 11, 748–754.

Hoffman, A. (2004). EMDR in the Treatment of Complex PTSD, EMDR International Association. Montreal, Quebec.

Hoffman, A. (2005). EMDR in der Behandlung psychotraumatischer Belastungssyndrome [EMDR therapy with posttraumatic stress syndromes]. Stuttgart, Germany: Thieme.

Kinowski, K. Best Foot Forward, presented at the 2002 EMDRIA Conference in San Diego.

Kitchur, M. (2000, December) The strategic developmental model for EMDR: A sequential treatment strategy for diverse populations, facilitative of developmental recapitulation, with implications for neurobiological maturation. The EMDRIA Newsletter, Special Edition, 4-10.

Kitchur, M. (2005). The Strategic Developmental Model. In R. Shapiro (Ed.), *EMDR Solutions: Pathways to Healing* (pp. 8-56). New York: W. W. Norton & Co.

Knipe, J. (2005) Targeting Positive Affect to Clear the Pain of Unrequited Love, Codependence, Avoidance and Procrastination, in Shapiro, R. (Ed.) *EMDR Solutions* New York: Norton.

Knipe, J. (2007) Loving Eyes: Procedures to Therapeutically Reverse Dissociative Processes while Preserving Emotional Safety, in Forgash, C. and Copeley, M. (Ed.s) <u>Healing the heart of trauma and dissociation</u>. Springer: New York.

Knipe, J. (2009a) Back of the Head Scale (BHS), The Method of Constant Installation of Present Orientation and Safety (CIPOS), in Luber, M., <u>*EMDR Scripted Protocols: Special Populations*</u>. New York: Springer.

Knipe, J. (2009b) Shame is my safe place: Adaptive Information Processing methods of resolving chronic shame-based depression, in Shapiro, R. (Ed.) *EMDR Solutions, Vol. II*, New York: Norton.

Korn, D. L., & Leeds, A. M. (2002). Preliminary evidence of efficacy for EMDR resource development and installation in the stabilization phase of treatment of complex posttraumatic stress disorder. *Journal of Clinical Psychology, 58*(12), 1465-1487.

Korn, D. L., Weir, J., & Rozelle, D. (2004). *Looking beyond the data: Clinical lessons learned from an EMDR treatment outcome study*, Session 321, EMDR International Association Conference. Montreal, Quebec: Nationwide Recording Services.

Leeds, A, Adaptive Information Processing, Attachment Theory and EMDR Case Conceptualization, Session 33 August 30, 2009 20th EMDRIA Conference Atlanta

Leeds, A, Lifting the Burden of Shame: Using EMDR Resource Installation to Resolve a Therapeutic Impasse, ed. Manfield, P., Extending EMDR: A Casebook of Innovative Applications, W. W. Norton, New York, 1998.

Leeds, A. M. (2009). A Guide to the Standard EMDR Protocols for Clinicians, Supervisors, and Consultants. New York: Springer Publishing.

Leeds, A. M., (2004) EMDR Treatment Made Simple, EMDRIA-Approved Continuing Education Workshop. May 22, 2004, Los Angeles.

Loftus, E. (1997), Creating False Memories, *Scientific American*, 277 (3),70-75.

Manfield, P.,(1992) *Split Self/ Split Object: Understanding and Treating Borderline, Narcissistic and Schizoid Disorders*, Jason Aronson Inc, New York,

Manfield, P. (1993, March). Using EMDR with difficult clients. Presentation at the EMDR Network Conference, Sunnyvale, CA.

Manfield, P. (1994, March). Personality disorders: Using EMDR with difficult clients. Presentation at the EMDR Network Conference, Sunnyvale, CA.

Manfield, P. (1995, June). Narcissistic disorders: Using EMDR with these difficult clients. Presentation at the EMDR Network Conference Santa Monica, CA.

Manfield, P. (Ed.),(1998) Extending EMDR: A Casebook of Innovative Applications, W. W. Norton, New York,.

Manfield, P. (1999, June). Double-blind alternating tone research. Presentation at the annual meeting of the EMDR International Association, Las Vegas, NV.

Manfield, P., & Snyker, E. (2002, June). Don't go with that!. Presentation at the annual meeting of the EMDR International Association, San Diego, CA.

Manfield, P. (Ed.),(2003) EMDR Casebook, W. W. Norton, New York,.

Manfield, P., (2005) Effective EMDR targeting with couples. Presentation at the annual meeting of the EMDR International Association, Seattle, WA., (2005, September).

Manfield, P., (2006) Effective EMDR targeting with couples. Presentation at the annual meeting of the EMDR International Association, Philadelphia, PA., (2006, September).

Manfield, P.,(2010) *Dyadic Resourcing: Building a Foundation for Processing Trauma*, Cornucopia Press, Albany, CA,

Manfield, P.,(2013) *EMDR Up Close: Subtleties of Trauma Processing*, Cornucopia Press, Albany, CA,

Manfield, P. (2014) EMDR Clinical Video Library, www.emdrclinicalvideos.com, JFK University, Pleasant Hill, CA

Maxfield, L., Manfield, P., Renssen, M. R., Smyth, N., Servan-Schreiber, D., & Bartone, P. M. (2001, June). The role of eye movements and other bilateral stimulation in EMDR. In R. Greenwald (Chair), Research Symposium II. Symposium conducted at the annual meeting of the EMDR International Association, Austin, TX.

McGaugh, J. L. (1989). Involvement of hormonal and neuromodulatory systems in the regulation of memory storage. Annual Review of Neuroscience, 2, 255–287.

McGaugh, J. L., & Roozendaal, B. (2002). Role of adrenal stress hormones in forming lasting memories in the brain. Current Opinions in Neurobiology, 12, 205–210.

Mileusnic, R., Lancashire, C. L., & Rose, S. P. R. (2005). Recalling an aversive experience by day-old chicks is not dependent on somatic protein synthesis. Learning & Memory, 12, 615–619.

Misanin, J. R., Miller, R. R., & Lewis, D. J. (1968). Retrograde amnesia produced by electroconvulsive shock following reactivation of a consolidated memory trace. Science, 16, 554–555.

Nader, K., Schafe, G. E., & LeDoux, J. E. (2000). Fear memories require protein synthesis in the amygdala for reconsolidation after retrieval. Nature, 406, 722–726.

Omaha, J., Psychotherapeutic Interventions for Emotion Regulation: EMDR and Bilateral Stimulation for Affect Management, NewYork: W.W. Norton, 2004

Parnell, Laurel, A Therapist's Guide to EMDR: Tools and Techniques for Successful Treatment, W.W. Norton, NY, NY, 2006.

Pedreira, M. E., Pérez-Cuesta, L. M., & Maldonado, H. (2002). Reactivation and reconsolidation of long-term memory in the crab Chasmagnathus: Protein synthesis requirement and mediation by NMDA-type glutamatergic receptors. Journal of Neuroscience, 22, 8305–8311.

Pedreira, M. E., Pérez-Cuesta, L. M., & Maldonado, H. (2004). Mismatch between what is expected and what actually occurs triggers memory reconsolidation or extinction. Learning & Memory, 11, 579–585.

Procrastination, in Shapiro, R. (Ed.) *EMDR Solutions* New York: Norton.

Propper, R., Pierce, J.P., Geisler, M.W., Christman, S.D., & Bellorado, N. (2007). Effect of bilateral eye movements on frontal interhemispheric gamma EEG coherence: Implications for EMDR therapy. *Journal of Nervous and Mental Disease*, 195, 785-788.

Rubin, R. D. (1976). Clinical use of retrograde amnesia produced by electroconvulsive shock: A conditioning hypothesis. Canadian Journal of Psychiatry, 21, 87–90.

Rubin, R. D., Fried, R., & Franks, C. M. (1969). New application of ECT. In R. D. Rubin & C. Franks (Eds.), Advances in behavior therapy,

Schmidt, S.J., *The Developmental Needs Meeting Strategy: A model for healing adults with childhood attachment wounds.* San Antonio, TX: DNMS Institute, 2006.

Schore, A. N. (2003a). *Affect dysregulation & disorders of the self* (1st ed.). New York: W.W. Norton.

Schore, A. N. (2003b). *Affect regulation & the repair of the self* (1st ed.). New York: W.W. Norton.

Shapiro, F. (1989a). Efficacy of the eye movement desensitization procedure in the treatment of traumatic memories. *Journal of Traumatic Stress Studies, 2,* 199–223.

Shapiro, F. (1989b). Eye movement desensitization: A new treatment for post-traumatic stress disorder. *Journal of Behavior Therapy and Experimental Psychiatry, 20,* 211–217.

Shapiro, F. (1991a). Eye movement desensitization and reprocessing procedure: From EMD to EMDR: A new treatment model for anxiety and related traumata. *Behavior Therapist, 14*, 133–135.

Shapiro, F. (1991b). Eye movement desensitization and reprocessing: A cautionary note. *Behavior Therapist, 14,* 188.

Shapiro, F. (1995). *Eye Movement Desensitization and Reprocessing, Basic Principles, Protocols and Procedures.* (1st ed.). New York: The Guilford Press.

Shapiro, F. (2001). *Eye Movement Desensitization and Reprocessing, Basic Principles, Protocols and Procedures.* (2nd ed.). New York: The Guilford Press.

Siegel, D. J. (1999). *The developing mind: Toward a neurobiology of interpersonal experience.* New York: Guilford.

Stickgold, R. (2002). EMDR: A putative neurobiological mechanism of action. *Journal of Clinical Psychology*, 58, 61-75.

Van der Hart, Onno, Ellert Nijenhuis, Kathy Steele, The Haunted Self: Structural Dissociation and the Treatment of Chronic Traumatization, W. W. Norton, N.Y., 2006

Van der Kolk, B; .J. Spinazzola; M. Blaustein.; J. Hopper.; E. Hopper.; D. Korn.; and W. Simpson et al (2007), A Randomized Clinical Trial of Eye Movement Desensitization and Reprocessing (EMDR), Fluoxetine, and Pill Placebo in the Treatment of Posttraumatic Stress Disorder: Treatment Effects and Long-Term Maintenance. *Journal of Clinical Psychiatry, 68*(1), 37-46.

Walker, Brakefield, Hobson, & Stickgold, (2003) Dissociable stages of jhuman memory consolidation and reconsolidation. Nature, 425, 616-620

Wesselmann, D, The Whole Parent : How to Become a Terrific Parent Even if You Didn't Have One, Perseus Publishing, NY, NY, 1991

Wildwind, L., "Treating Chronic Depression," Paper presented at the annual EMDR Conference, Sunnyvale, CA, April, 1992.

About the author:

Philip Manfield, PhD, has been a psychotherapist in private practice in the San Francisco Bay Area for 40 years. He has been involved for the past 20 years in EMDR training as a facilitator, presenter, and later a trainer in North and South America, Europe, Asia, Australia and the Middle East. He is an EMDRIA-approved consultant and instructor, and is EMDRIA Northern California Regional Coordinator. Dr. Manfield is the author of *Split Self/Split Object* (1992, Aronson) and editor of two casebooks, *Extending EMDR: A Casebook of Innovative Applications* (W.W. Norton, 1998) and *EMDR Casebook* (W.W. Norton, 2003). Prior to the publication of *EMDR Up Close: Subtleties of Trauma Processing* his most recent book was *Dyadic Resourcing: Creating a Foundation for Processing Trauma* (Cornucopia Publishers, 2010). John F. Kennedy University is currently sponsoring a website with 29 full clinical videos of his work (www.emdrclinicalvideos.com).